Back Bar Breweriana

A Guide to
Advertising
Beer Statues
and
Beer Shelf Signs

with

1993-94 Price Guide

© Copyright 1992
2nd Printing 1994

By George Baley

Published By

L-W Book Sales
P.O. Box 69
Gas City, IN 46933

9257692

Cover Design: Jamison Miller
Interior Design: Jamison Miller

B

Back Bar Breweriana

*A Collector's Guide to Beer Statues
and Chalk Shelf Signs*

George J. Baley

*This project would not have been accomplished without the help of
John Beran, Ken Hostetter, Don Schultz, Tom Snyder, Bill Taylor,
Bob Arnold, Ron Kitka, Joseph Borowitz, the Oldenberg Brewery
and the late Rod Everett who permitted their collections to be photographed or assisted with the price guide.*

*Inquiries and comments about Back Bar Breweriana may be
directed to the author at:*

*George J. Baley
P.O. Box 2043
Portage, MI 49081*

.....................Table of Contents.....................

PRICE GUIDE DISCLAIMER

The Price Guide featured in the rear of this book reflects only estimated values suggested by persons educated in the Beer Statue field. Therefore, L-W Book Sales will not be responsible for any losses in the case of purchasing or sale of any Beer Statue or Beer Shelf Sign.

INTRODUCTION

HISTORY

The origin of the true beer statue is generally placed in the era of the 1930's upon the repeal of Prohibition. Most widely used as point-of-purchase advertising through most of the 1960's and early 70's, few companies (Lowenbrau and Rolling Rock) employ such advertising aides anymore.

Typically statues were provided at no charge to bars, saloons and tap rooms for display at the back of the bar, in plain view of customers, as they sat on a stool and enjoyed their favorite brew. A more exact definition of what constitutes this family of collectibles is often debated by serious collectors because of the natural progression from the 'true' statue through their nearest neighbors the chalk shelf sign, figural foam scraper holders and lastly the chalk wall plaque.

BREWERY THEMES

Breweries often featured a unique character that was integrated into its other advertising schemes.

Men - Men were often featured with brands such as Pfeiffer's Johnnie Pfeiffer (429 - 439); Blatz skater (37); and waiter (62); Schmidt's bartenders (494- 498); Pabst's boxer (408 - 410, 419 - 420) and bartender (411 - 418); Gettleman's Fritzie (189 - 190); Drewry's Mountie (110 - 128); and Falstaff's John Falstaff (155 - 163).

Animals - Animal themes were common as depicted by Goebel's Brewster the Rooster (195 - 198) and Frankenmuth's Dog (179 - 182). Horses were popular with Drewry, Old Shay (390 - 393) and Rolling Rock (472 - 481), while bears adorned Fehr (168), Hamm (212 - 226) and Oertels (355).

Bar Scenes - Bar scenes from Burkhardts (93 - 94), Iron City (268 - 270), Tech (520 - 521) and Yusay (554 - 556) used the same basic design modified slightly in width, number of patrons and color scheme. Bartenders and waiters adorned the themes of many beer statues.

Women - Women were not commonly featured in BBB and have been limited to the classic Blatz girl (33 - 34), the Sterling Bell girl (509 - 512), the Miller girl (329 - 337), the Pabst (405) woman (reported to be Doris Day) and the Fehr (169)/West Virginia lady's hand holding a bottle and a few others.

Children - Children were sometimes used on some brands like Heineken's (248 - 251), Sterling (511) and Grolsch (202), much to the dismay of groups against drinking by young people.

COMPILATION OF BBB LISTING

The items shown in this book represent a cross section of some of the finest collections in the United States. As the project proceeded, it became clear that a total listing was not within our grasp and that some logical cut-off would be necessary. Thus, at this time, over 600 items have been depicted with another dozen photographed, but having missed the cut-off date for publication.

Since it is our plan to generate a second volume which will contain new additions including chalk wall plaques, your participation is most welcome. Please drop me a line if you have an item or comment to include in the future volume.

CLASSIFICATION OF BBB

We will confine our presentation to BBB represented by three dimensional statues, chalk shelf signs and a few 'kissing cousins' to the statues and will save for a later volume chalk plaques, wood and plastic shelf signs, traditional wall hangings and non-figural foam scraper holders. No liquor or wine statues are shown.

Under each picture is listed a sequential number corresponding to the price guide in the back of the book. Next to the identifying number is the brand of beer represented, followed by the city and state where brewed and the estimated date of issuance. The second line contains the approximate height in inches, the four most prevalent colors in descending order and last, the material (s) of construction. The far right portion of the second line contains a key word (s) for certain items to describe their relative rarity, authenticity or other specific characteristics.

While the intent of most BBB were as advertising gimmicks, many served a second purpose. The 1930's and 1940's were an era when foam scrapers were used to level the 'head' of a freshly drawn glass of beer. Schmidts (494-499), Piels (446) and Edelbrau (139) provided a place for a glass or cup to hold the scrapers. Health concerns in most states over transfer of germs from one customer to another eventually banned the foam scraper and thus this sub category of statues. Blatz introduced an egg (hopefully hard boiled) roller statue (39) complete with salt and pepper shaker. Ashtrays were integrated into the design of statues such as Old Vienna (402), Oertels (360) and Frankenmuth (183-186). The Frankenmuth man statue was actually designed to be an ashtray.

MATERIALS OF CONSTRUCTION

Often referred to as "chalks" by the avid collector, beer statues have over the years been fabricated from a wide variety of materials.

Since most statue manufacturing companies employed sculptors to design their products, it is reasonable that chalk was the most popular material of construction. In reviewing the statues shown in this book, the predominance (about 65%) were chalk. Commonly referred to as *Plaster of Paris* it was similar to that used to plaster walls in a home. Commercially manufactured chalk statues were usually re-enforced through the addition of chemical strengthening agents, horse hair and metal rods designed to increase the overall strength of the statue. In addition to chalk, common materials included rubber, metal and plastic. Less common materials included glass, foam, papier mache and wood.

Normally the condition one finds BBB in is related to the materials of construction. Chalk statues typically encountered the greatest exposure to damage, breakage and the elements. It is common to find cracks, chips and missing parts from many chalk statues. The metal center re-enforcing rods used in many statues tended to rust over the years and resulted in crack formation. Metal, plastic, glass and wood statues, if unbroken often have maintained their near original structure, but likely have encountered some fading and scratching. Most rubber statues show various degrees of deformation, sagging and fading and are therefore the least likely to have survived in pristine condition. Exposure to light or excessive heat degrades rubber quickly and therefore protection from excessive conditions is important.

RESTORATION

It is the general consensus of seasoned collectors that restoration of a statue or a shelf sign does <u>not</u> significantly enhance its dollar value. Most collectors prefer to have an original unretouched piece, even if minor damage is evident.

Restoration i.e. repainting should be attempted only by someone familiar with mimicking the true colors used in the original paint process. Most restorers have found that model airplane paint (Testors) closely approximates the original finish and appearance of most chalk statues. A clear spray finish will preserve the final surface. Water based paints, unless protected with a clear coat, should never be used. Minor touch up can often be accomplished by using a Sharpie brand marking pen to darken reds, green, browns or black. Pastel colors were almost never used and should be avoided in any repainting.

Large cracks which affect the stability of a statue can be injected with Epoxy cement to strengthen loose sections.

Reconstruction of chalk parts can be accomplished through the use of *Plaster of Paris*, patching compound or fiberglass "Bondo" followed by careful sanding and painting. Again, major restoration of the rarer statues should be left to the professional.

H

PRICING STATUES AND CHALK SHELF SIGNS

The value of a particular statue is dependent upon three criteria: rarity, quality of detail/design and condition. Even the rarest of statues has little value unless it is in fairly good condition.

Rarity - Rarity is a difficult attribute to determine since what may be rare in one part of the country is common in another part. With the exception of a few national brands like Blatz, Pabst or Miller most breweries issued their beer in relatively well defined regions of the country.

It has been suggested that many of the rarer items were issued in relatively low numbers. Typically a manufacturer of statues would make limited runs of a few dozen. Most collectors agree that to be 'rare', 6 or less must be know to exist. Thus, one may assume that the reason some statues are 'one-of-a-kind' is because of this limited distribution or the financial status of the brewery. On the other hand, the Plasto Manufacturing Company which was the largest fabricator of statues, produced a minimum of 500 statues of any type and often, as with the small Johnnie Pfeiffer (429 - 431), would receive orders for thousands at a time!!! Few statues produced by Plasto were ever sold to the breweries for more than $10, although today some Plasto statues command ten times that amount or more.

Design - Great debate exists on what is the most attractive statue made. Certainly brands like the A-1 (1), Bosch (65 - 67), Grand Prize (200), Krantz' (280), Poth (455), Yankee (552), Phoenix (440), Anteck (14), Old Brew (367) and the Van Merritt (535) rank at or near the top. Beauty and design are in the eyes of the beholder!

Condition - The condition of an item will dramatically affect its value. The section of Grading deals with reductions in price based on condition. As with any collectable, accurate grading is a very difficult task and varies widely.

PRICE GUIDE

The dollar value for each item has been described by a price range established through consultation with many serious collectors who provided access to their collections for photography and others familiar with the hobby. The author appreciates the openness and honesty of those who contributed their time to this project.

A range was employed to provide latitude and judgement with regards to a particular item. The price range is for a Grade 1 (near mint) item. Lower or off grade items will decrease in value based on their overall condition.

I

Statues with an estimated value in excess of $450 (Grade 1) have been designated as "450+" and the final value will depend upon condition, recent discoveries and collector interest.

COMMENTS SECTION

Pertinent comments assisting in the description of many items have been included below the picture in the height/color/composition line.

Rare - A statue received a "rare" designation when 6 or less have been reported, as of this printing. It is likely that with the publishing of this book, many rare statues will come out of hiding and their "rarity" will be decreased. It should be noted that rarity and value or price were not related when establishing the price guide. Thus, a "rare" statue could have a relatively low $ value while a more common one may actually be valued in the hundreds of dollars.

Repainted Statues - Repainted statues are differentiated from restored statues in that over the years many fine statues have been altered in colors totally different from the original. The white Frankenmuth dog (179), Bergermeister (92) and Tech (520) are known repaints. This is another reason why serious collectors prefer to obtain statues in their original condition, usually decrease the value of a restored statue or avoid it totally.

Altered Statues - Many times authentic statues were reconfigured by non-beer drinkers and used as decorations in their homes. The most common examples of this are statues which depict horses as the main theme. Many Drewry 'mounties' and Old Shays have been found with any reference to beer having been removed. The value of an altered statue will depend upon its rarity and whether restoration is really worth it. Normally altered statues should be in the 25 - 33% range of the low book.

Prototypes - Often breweries experimented with 'prototypes' before choosing one style or character for their logo, symbol, or mascot. This was true of an Old Reading (389), Patrick Henry (423) and Miller girl (330). The value of a prototype depends on the brewery and the general interest among collectors for that item.

Reproductions - Reproductions are mentioned to alert collectors of a very real, but limited trend in the hobby. At this printing only the 'Oertels Family' of statues is known to being counterfeited and is restricted to the "Howdy Doody" (356), all hands (363 - 365), ashtray (360) and most recently the Owl (357). These are easily detected by their dull finish and relatively soft chalk surfaces. Unless an original statue has been repainted, a dead give away to a reproduction is to determine if the bottom surface was painted.

Original chalk statues were almost never painted on the bottom, but <u>may</u> have been felt padded. Also, very <u>few</u> original statues were hollow, so if a solid one and a hollow one are found of the same item, the solid one is most likely a reproduction.

The price shown for a statue is what an original, authentic statue is worth. A copy should never be purchased for an amount more than 1/3 of 1/2 of the low price range. Thus, the price for a reproduction like the Oertel's owl (357) is perhaps $50 while an original still commands $136-200.

Fake (not reproductions) - Fake statues are relatively uncommon and often are the result of misinterpretation or misrepresentation of a non brewery item as BBB. The Schlitz Malt Liquor bull (491) and Pabst (418) are known personally by the author to be fake. The authenticity of the West Pennsylvania Moose (541), as a beer statue is also in question, since no brewery is known to have been named West Pennsylvania! A good rule of thumb is that if an unbranded item is not known to be from a specific brewery, let it lie unless very inexpensive.

The value of a fake statue is virtually nil to the serious collector and should be looked upon as a novelty at best.

Novelty Items - Novelty items are so designated because it is unlikely they were actually issued by the brewery being depicted. For example the Coor's (103), Corona (104) and all <u>small</u> Lone Star armadillos (296 - 298) and dancing man/woman (299 - 300) are believed to be novelties. They were probably sold to novelty shops in the area where the beer was sold. On a recent vacation to Southern California, many versions of the Corona and small Lone Star statues were observed and could be purchased for $5-10 each!

Beware of the Future - Breweriana collectors for years have been weary of the con artist and for the most part with the exception of recent counterfeiting of old rare beer bottle labels have been sheltered from deceit. Beer cans, other than "rolled" cans are difficult to economically reproduce. Chalk statues however present an opportunity as we have seen with the Oertels for quick profit. It is likely that in time some unscrupulous person will begin fabricating counterfeit BBB. This is especially true when statues are valued in the hundreds of dollars. It is likely that copyright laws are being violated and appropriate action may be taken against future counterfeiting. It would be nice if the counterfeiters would simply mark their items as "Authentic Reproduction". Buyer beware!!!!!!

What About Size?

The smallest known statue may be the tiny Toby (526) man which measures a mere 3" while the tallest depicted here is the 45" Schlitz man (487) with the world on his shoulder. The largest known statue is probably the Black Horse Ale cast iron decoration in front of the brewery in Canada, but not pictured in this book. A tall Styrofoam Hamm's Bear is very popular with collectors although its size can be a problem if space is a concern.

Original BBB Manufacturers

Over 25 companies are known to have fabricated statues and chalk shelf signs. Chalk statues often include the manufacturers name and sometimes city, usually on the side or back. The largest and most prolific producer over the years was the Plasto Manufacturing Company of Chicago. They started out in 1944 and manufactured statues in chalk, metal (Pabst) and plastic into the late 70's. In addition to statues they made lamps, lamp shades and other novelty items and finally ceased operations in 1983. Another company known for producing high quality and detailed items was the W.J. Smith Company of Louisville, Kentucky. Many of the finer detail liquor statues were made by the Smith Company.

Other manufacturers include:

Alexander Corp.	Philadelphia, PA.
Bosograf, E.M.	Chicago, IL.
Central States Specialty Co.	
Embossograph Display Mfg. Co.	Chicago, IL.
Florence Art Inc.	San Francisco, CA.
Golden, B.J. & Co.	Pittsburg, PA.
Golden, W.J. (Elmond Original)	Pittsburg, PA.
Handicraft (Tili Mac)	Los Angeles, CA.
Kolorgraph Inc.	Louisville, KY.
Louis Compo Prod.	Detroit, MI.
Martelle-Lamb Inc.	Louisville, KY.
Modern Tuscany Art Co.	Philadelphia, PA.
Phase Four Products	New York, NY.
Plasto Manufacturing Co.	Chicago, IL.
Schultz, & Co., Thomas	
Silvestri Bros. Co.	
Smith, W.J.	Louisville, KY.
Timely Products	Des Moines, IA.

DATING OF BBB

Statues from a particular brewery often employed a similar theme used for other advertising. It is therefore possible to date items, by referring to printed ads and literature. A copyright date is sometimes present on the statue itself which is helpful. The Beer Can Collectors Bible issued in the 1970's can be a valuable reference to approximate the age of statues since can dates were included for companies that canned beer. By noting fine details of a can for example, the statues age can be approximated. Many statues utilized a can or bottle which any include a copyright date or brewery address which will assist in dating the item.

Books like American Breweries by Don Bull or Who's Who in Brewing can be helpful in establishing when a particular brewery was in business and the brands they produced.

Publications from the Beer Can Collectors of America (BCCA), National Association of Brewery Advertising (NABA), American Breweriana Association (ABA) and the East Coast Breweriana Association (ECBA) are all excellent sources of detailed information.

GRADING OF BBB

The percentages (%) shown below should be applied to the price guide value for each item.

Grade 1: (100% +)
Pristine condition, free from chips, cracks, fading or missing parts.

Grade 2: (80 - 100%)
Very minor scratches, no chips, cracks or missing parts.

Grade 3: (60 - 80%)
Minor chips, no cracks, fading or missing parts. Professionally repaired and repainted statues are Grade 3.

Grade 4: (30 - 60%)
Minor chips or cracks, restorable missing parts, slight fading. Non professionally repainted statues generally will be classified as Grade 4.

Grade 5: (0 - 30%)
Large chips, cracks and fading; restorable missing parts. Reserved for common statues of extremely poor condition and collectable only as "place holders" until something better turns up.

Abbreviation Code

Color Codes

The coding system below has been used to indicate the four primary colors in approximate descending order.

Bl	= Blue		M	= Maroon
Bk	= Black		O	= Orange
Bn	= Brown		P	= Pink
Br	= Brass		R	= Red
Cr	= Cream		Si	= Silver
Cl	= Clear plastic		T	= Tan
Co	= Copper		Vi	= Violet
F	= Flesh tone		W	= White
Gd	= Gold		Wd	= Wood
Gn	= Green		Y	= Yellow
Gy	= Gray			

Brand = Brand of beer that the Statue or Shelf Sign represents.

Brewery = Name of company that sold the brand of beer. (Noted in Price Guide)

Year = Year of issuance. (estimated)

Height = Height in inches. (including bottle of present)

Composition

C	= Chalk
Cl	= Cloth
Co	= Composite (tar-like substance)
Cr	= Ceramic
F	= Foam
G	= Glass
M	= Metal
P	= Plastic
Pa	= Paper or papier mache
R	= Rubber
S	= Stuffed
W	= Wood

Canada:	CN
Great Britain:	GB
Denmark:	DM
Holland:	HD
Japan:	JA

BEER STATUES

1. A-1, Phoenix, AZ. 1953.
   11 - Y, Bn, Bk, R - C.   Rare (Clock/Lights)

2. Acme, Los Angeles, CA. 1940.
   7 - Cr, Y, W, R - C.

3. Acme, Los Angeles, CA. 1940.
   7 - W, R, Bl - C.

4. Acme, Los Angeles, CA. 1940.
   13 - W, Bn, Cr, R - C.   Rare

5. Alpine, Grand Rapids, MI. 1955.
   11 - Gn, F, C - C.

6. Altes, Detroit, MI. 1953.
   9.5 - W, Gd, R - C.

7. Altes, Detroit, MI. 1953.
11 - W, Gd, R - C.

8. Altes, Detroit, MI. 1953.
11 - W, Gd, R - C.

9. Altes, Detroit, MI. 1953.
14 - F, Gn, Y - C.

10. Altes, Detroit, MI. 1953.
14 - F, Gn, Y - C.

11. Altes, Detroit, MI. 1953.
10.5 - F, Gn, Y - C.

12. Altes, Detroit, MI. 1953.
10.5 - F, Gn, Y - C.

13. American, Baltimore, MD. 1958.
    8.5 - W, R, Bk - C.

14. Anteck, Carnegie, PA. 1939.
    26 - Cr, Bn, Bk, Gn - R.   Rare

15. Ballantine, Newark, NJ. 1951.
    6.5 - W, R, Gd - W.

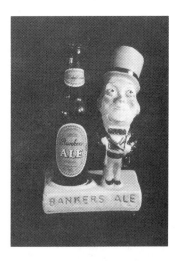

16. Bankers, San Francisco, CA. 1948.
    11 - Cr, Gy, R - C.   Rare

17. Batholomay, Rochester, NY. 1915.
    5 - Br - M.   Rare

18. Ben Brew, Columbus, OH. 1952.
    11 - R, W, Bl, Bk - C.   Rare

19. Black Horse, Montreal, CN. 1960.
12 - Bk, W, Si, Gn - CRM.

20. Black Horse, Montreal, CN. 1960.
14.5 - Bk, Gr, W - R.

21. Black Horse, Montreal, CN. 1960.
10. 5 - Bk, Gd - C.

22. Black Horse, Montreal, CN. 1960.
11.5 - Bk, Gd - C.

23. Black Horse, Montreal, CN. 1960.
11 - Bk, W, Gn, Gd - C.

24. Black Horse, Montreal, CN. 1960.
12 - Bk, W, Si, Gn - CRM.

25. Black Horse, Montreal, CN. 1960.
    19 - W, Bk - C.

26. Black Horse, Dunkirk, NY. 1960.
    10 - Bk, Gn, W, Y - C.

27. Black Horse, Montreal, CN. 1960.
    15 - Bk, Gd - C.

28. Black Horse, Montreal, CN. 1960.
    10.5 - Bk, Gn, Cr - R.

29. Black Horse, Dunkirk, NY. 1960.
    8.5 - Bk, W - P.

30. Black Horse, Dunkirk, NY. 1960.
    8.5 - Bk, W - P.

31. Black Horse, Dunkirk, NY. 1960.
    8 - Bk, W - P.

32. Black Label, Cleveland, OH. 1968.
    15.5 - Bk, W, Cr, R - CPa.

33. Blatz, Milwaukee, WI. 1936.
    18.5 - Bn, Cr, R - C.

34. Blatz, Milwaukee, WI. 1984.
    20 - Gd - P.   Lights

35. Blatz, Milwaukee, WI. 1968.
    17 - Gd, Bk, F, Bn - MP.

36. Blatz, Milwaukee, WI. 1968.
    17 - Gd, Bk, F, Bn - MP.

37. Blatz, Milwaukee, WI. 1968.
18.5 - W, Bk, Bn, Si - M.

39. Blatz, Milwaukee, WI. 1968.
28 - Bl, Bk, W, Y - M.

40. Blatz, Milwaukee, WI. 1968.
16 - Gn, W, Bn, Bl - M.

41. Blatz, Milwaukee, WI. 1968.
13.3 - Bn, Gy, R, W - C.

42. Blatz, Milwaukee, WI. 1968.
13.3 - Bn, Gy, R, W - C.

43. Blatz, Milwaukee, WI. 1968.
11 - F, Bn, Gd, R - MP.

44. Blatz, Milwaukee, WI. 1968.
    14 - Bn, Y, Bl, F - PG.

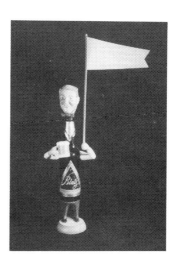

45. Blatz, Milwaukee, WI. 1968.
    14 - Bn, Y, Bl, F - PG.

46. Blatz, Milwaukee, WI. 1968.
    11.5 - Bl, W, Bn, F - MP.

47. Blatz, Milwaukee, WI. 1968.
    11.5 - Bl, W, Bn, F - MP.

48. Blatz, Milwaukee, WI. 1968.
    11.5 - Bl, W, Bn, F - MP.

49. Blatz, Milwaukee, WI. 1968.
    9 - Gd, Bn, Bk - MP.

50. Blatz, Milwaukee, WI. 1968.
17 - R, Bn, W, Bl - M.

51. Blatz, Milwaukee, WI. 1968.
17 - R, Bn, W, Bl - M.   Lights

52. Blatz, Milwaukee, WI. 1968.
10.5 - Bn, Gd, W, R - M.

53. Blatz, Milwaukee, WI. 1968.
10.5 - Bn, Gd, W, R - M.

54. Blatz, Milwaukee, WI. 1968.
10.5 - Bn, Gd, W, R - M.

55. Blatz, Milwaukee, WI. 1968.
16 - Bn, F, W, R - M.

56. Blatz, Milwaukee, WI. 1953.
    7 - Bk, F, W, R - W.

57. Blatz, Milwaukee, WI. 1960.
    7 - Bk, F, W, R - W.

58. Blatz, Milwaukee, WI. 1953.
    7.5 - W, Y, Bk, Gn - M.

59. Blatz, Milwaukee, WI. 1953.
    7 - Bk, F, W, R - W.

60. Blatz, Milwaukee, WI. 1960.
    11 - Bk, W, Gd, R - MP.   Lights & Moves

61. Blatz, Milwaukee, WI. 1968.
    9 - Gd, Bn, Bk - PM.

BEER STATUES

62. Blatz, Milwaukee, WI. 1968.
16 - Gd, Bn, R, W - M.

63. Blatz, Milwaukee, WI. 1968.
16 - Gd, Bn, R, W - M.

64. Blitz, Portland, OR. 1951.
9.75 - W, Gn, O, Y - C.

65. Bosch, Houghton, MI. 1959.
10 - Cr, Gn, R, F - C.   Rare

66. Bosch, Houghton, MI. 1959.
10 - R, W, Gr - C.

67. Bosch, Houghton, MI. 1959.
6.5 - Bl, Bn, R, Gr - C.

68. Boston Light Ale, Boston, MA. 1938.
22 - Bk, W, R - RG.   Rare/Lights

69. Boswell, Quebec, CN. 1955.
15 - Bn, Bk, W, Gd - R.   Rare

70. Brading's Cincinnati, Toronto, CN. 1963.
15.5 - Bn, Bk, F, W - R.   Rare

71. Breidt's, Elizabeth, NJ. 1934.
17.5 - Bl, R, Bk, Y - C.   Rare

72. Bruck's, Cincinnati, OH. 1955.
10 - Bl, Y, Si, R - C.

73. Buckeye, Cincinnati, OH. 1957.
11.5 - W, Bk, R, Bl - RPa.

74. Bud Light, St. Louis, MO. 1987.
    15 - Bl, W, Bk, R - P.

75. Budweiser, St. Louis, MO. 1985.
    7 - Gd - M.

76. Budweiser. 1970.
    7 - Cr - C.   Novelty

77. Budweiser. 1970.
    7 - R - C.   Novelty

78. Budweiser, St. Louis, MO. 1959.
    7 - Bk, F, W, R - W.

79. Budweiser, St. Louis, MO. 1980.
    18 - R, Bk, F - S.

80. Budweiser. 1989.
    7 - Gy, Bl, W, Bk - Cr.   Novelty

81. Budweiser, St. Louis, MO. 1975.
    21 - Gd, Bk - P.

82. Bull Dog, San Francisco, CA. 1951.
    8 - W, R, Y - Cr.   Rare

83. Bull Dog, San Francisco, CA. 1951.
    8 - W, Y, Bk, R - Cr.   Rare

84. Bull Dog, San Francisco, CA. 1951.
    8 - W, Gy - Cr.   Rare

85. Burger, Cincinnati, OH. 1952.
    15 - Bn, R, W, Bk - WR.

86. Burger, Cincinnati, OH. 1959.
15 - Bn, W, R, Bk - FR.   Rare

87. Burger, Cincinnati, OH. 1963.
15 - Bn, Gn, Bk, W - FP.   Rare

88. Burger, Cincinnati, OH. 1971.
8.5 - W, Bl - Cr.

89. Burger, Cincinnati, OH. 1971.
8.5 - W, Bl - Cr.

90. Burgermeister, San Francisco, CA. 1953.
16 - Gd - C.

91. Burgermeister, San Francisco, CA. 1953.
16 - Gd, Bn - C.

92. Burgermeister, San Francisco, CA. 1953.
    16 - Bl, Bn, W, Y - C.   Repainted #90

93. Burkhardt's, Akron, OH. 1953.
    8.5 - Cr, R, Gd - C.

94. Burkhardt's, Akron, OH. 1953.
    8.5 - Bn, W, R - C.   Repainted #93

95. Busch, St. Louis, MO. 1970.
    10 - Si, Gd, W - P.   Lights

96. Calgary, Calgary, CN. 1960.
    16 - Gd, Bl, R, W - F.   Lights

97. Canadian Ace, Chicago, IL. 1955.
    10 - Cr, Gn, Y, R - C.

98. Carlsberg, Copenhagen, DM. 1974.
6.5 - W, Gn, R - Cr.

99. Chief Oshkosh, Oshkosh, WI. 1957.
10.3 - Gr, Bl - C.

100. Chief Oshkosh, Oshkosh, WI. 1957.
8 - Bn, Bk, R, W - C.

101. Cooper's, Philadelphia, PA. 1940.
15 - W, Bk, Bn, Gd - C.

102. Cooper's, Philadelphia, PA. 1940.
15 - W, Bk, Bn, Gd - C.

103. Coor's. 1965.
6 - Cr, R, Y, Bk - C.   Fake

BEER STATUES

104. Corona. 1980.
  11 - Bn, Y, Bk - C.   Novelty

105. Crystal Rock, Cleveland, OH. 1955.
  13.5 - Bl, W, Bz, F - C.   Rare

106. Dakota, Bismark, SD. 1959.
  14 - F, Bn, W - C.   Rare

107. Delta, Escanaba, MI. 1940.
  8.5 - Gd, R - R.   Rare

108. Diplomat, New Brittain, CT. 1953.
  14 - F, Bk, R - C.   Rare

109. Double Diamond, Burton-on-Trent, GB. 1955.
  8.5 - Bk, Y, F, R - Cr.

110. Drewrys, South Bend, IN. 1940.
14 - Gy, Bn, Bl, W - C.

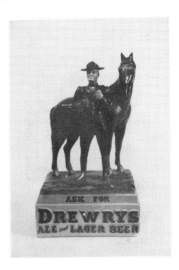

111. Drewrys, South Bend, IN. 1940.
15 - Si, Bn, R, Bk - C.

112. Drewrys, South Bend, IN. 1947.
15 - Gd - C.   Lights

113. Drewrys, South Bend, IN. 1947.
23 - Y, Bn, R, Bl - C.   Rare

114. Drewrys, South Bend, IN. 1955.
14.5 - Cr, R, Bk, Bn - C. Lights

115. Drewrys, South Bend, IN. 1947.
11 - Bn, R, Y, W - C.   Lights

116. Drewrys, South Bend, IN. 1947.
11 - Bn, R, Y, W - C.

117. Drewrys, South Bend, IN. 1955.
11 - Bn, R, Y, W - C.

118. Drewrys, South Bend, IN. 1955.
11 - Bn, R, Y, W - C.

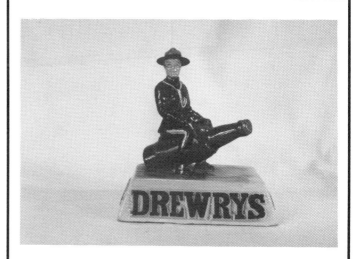

119. Drewrys, South Bend, IN. 1955.
6.75 - Cr, R, Bl, Bn - C.

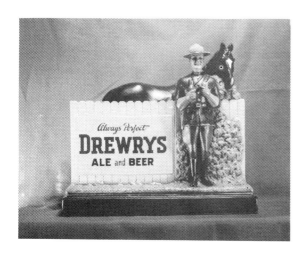

120. Drewrys, South Bend, IN. 1940.
13 - Cr, Bk, R, Bl - C.   Rare

121. Drewrys, South Bend, IN. 1955.
7.25 - Cr, R, Bl, Bn - C.

122. Drewrys, South Bend, IN. 1955.
7.25 - Cr, R, Bl, Bn - C.

123. Drewrys, South Bend, IN. 1955.
7.25 - Cr, R, Bl, Bn - C.

124. Drewrys, South Bend, IN. 1955.
7.25 - Cr, R, Bl, Bn - C.

125. Drewrys, South Bend, IN. 1955.
7.25 - Bn, R, Y, W - C.

126. Drewrys, South Bend, IN. 1947.
7 - Bn, R, Bl, T - C.

127. Drewrys, South Bend, IN. 1955.
7.5 - Cr, R, Bl, Bn - C.

128. Drewrys, South Bend, IN. 1955.
     7.5 - Cr, R, Bl, Bn - C.

129. Drewrys, South Bend, IN. 1957.
     9.5 - W, Bl, R, Bk - P.

130. Drewrys, South Bend, IN. 1957.
     11 - W, Bl, R, Bk - P.

131. Drewrys, South Bend, IN. 1955.
     7.5 - Y, W, Bk, F - C.

132. DuBois, DuBois, PA. 1960.
     16 - Cr, R - C.

133. DuBois, DuBois, PA. 1960.
     16 - Cr, Bn, R, Bk - C.

134. DuBois, DuBois, PA. 1965.
  12 - Gd, Y, Bk, W - C.   Rare

135. Duquesne, Pittsburg, PA. 1956.
  10.8 - Cr, R, Bl, Gd - C.

136. Duquesne, Pittsburg, PA. 1956.
  14.5 - Bn, R, W - C.

137. Duquesne, Pittsburg, PA. 1956.
  8 - Bn, Si - C.

138. Duquesne, Pittsburg, PA. 1950.
  12 - Bn, W - W.

139. Edelbrau, Los Angeles, CA. 1972.
  11 - W, Gn - C.

140. Eifenbrau, WI. 1938.
     24 - Bn, R, W - C.   Rare

141. Erin Brew, Cleveland, OH. 1958.
     8 - Bn, Gn, W, Y - C.

142. Erin Brew, Rochester, NY. 1958.
     12.5 - Si, Gn, R - C.

143. Erin Brew, Cleveland, OH. 1952.
     8 - W, Gn, R, Y - C.

144. Erin Brew, Cleveland, OH. 1952.
     8 - Bn, Bk, W - C.

145. Erin Brew, Rochester, NY. 1952.
     12.5 - Bl, Gn, Y - C.

146. Erlanger, Philadelphia, PA. 1948.
10 - Bk, W, R, Gd - C.   Rare

147. Esslinger, Philadelphia, PA. 1953.
19 - R, Cr, F, Bk - C.   Rare

148. Falls City, Louisville, KY. 1976.
11 - R, W - C.

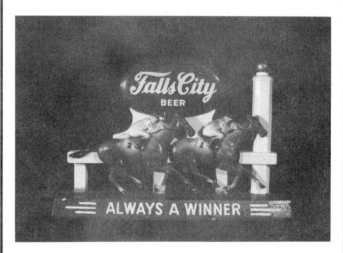

149. Falls City, Louisville, KY. 1953.
11 - W, Gn, Bn, R - C.

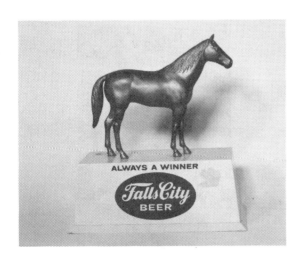

150. Falls City, Louisville, KY. 1972.
10 - W, Gd, R, Bk - P.

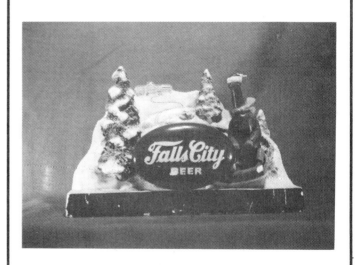

151. Falls City, Louisville, KY. 1953.
8.5 - W, R, Gn, Bn - C.   Rare

152. Falls City, Louisville, KY. 1951.
    8.5 - W, Bl, Gd, R - C.   Rare

153. Falls City, Louisville, KY. 1970.
    14 - Gd, Bn, Cr, R - RW.

154. Falls City, Louisville, KY. 1970.
    21 - Bn, W, R, Bl - S.

155. Falstaff, St. Louis, MO. 1954.
    16.8 - Bn, M, Gd, Gn - C.

156. Falstaff, St. Louis, MO. 1954.
    16.5 - Gd - R.

157. Falstaff, St. Louis, MO. 1954.
    11.8 - Bn, M, Gd, Gn - C.

158. Falstaff, St. Louis, MO. 1954.
16.5 - M, Bn, Gn, Gd - C.

159. Falstaff, St. Louis, MO. 1938.
21 - Y, R, Gn, Bk - C.

160. Falstaff, St. Louis, MO. 1938.
21 - Y, R, Gn, Bk - C.

161. Falstaff, St. Louis, MO. 1954.
8.5 - Bn, R, F, Gn - C.

162. Falstaff, St. Louis, MO. 1954.
9.5 - Gd, R - C.

163. Falstaff, St. Louis, MO. 1954.
9.5 - Gd - F.

164. Falstaff. 1954.
   5.5 - Bn, W, Bk, R - C.   Novelty

165. Falstaff. 1954.
   5.5 - Gy - C.   Novelty

166. Falstaff. 1954.
   5.5 - Gd - C.   Novelty

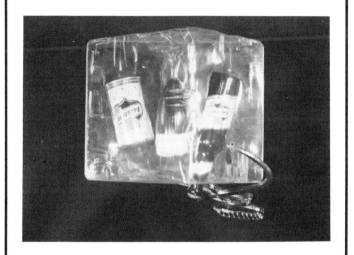

167. Falstaff, St. Louis, MO. 1960.
   10 - Cl, Gd, W, Y - P.

168. Fehr's, Cincinnati, OH. 1953.
   15.5 - W, R, G, Bk - C.

169. Fehr's, Cincinnati, OH. 1953.
   15.5 - Cr, R - C.   Rare

170. Fesenmeier, Huntington, WV. 1962.
10 - W, Bl, R, Gd - C.

171. Fidelio, New York, NY. 1940.
9.5 - Bn, Bl, Gn - C.   Rare

172. Fitgers, Duluth, MN. 1940.
8 - Br, O, Gy - C.

173. Fort Pitt, Pittsburg, PA. 1954.
13 - Cr, Bl, Y - C.

174. Fox DeLuxe, Chicago, IL. 1949.
16 - R, Cr, Bn - C.

175. Fox DeLuxe, Grand Rapids, MI. 1949.
16 - R, Cr, Bn - C.

176. Fox DeLuxe, Chicago, IL. 1949.
11.5 - R, Cr, Bn - C.

177. Fox Head 400, Waukesha, WI. 1949.
9.75 - Cr, R, Gd, Bk - C.

178. Fox Head 400, Waukesha, WI. 1954.
7 - Bk, F, W - W.

179. Frankenmuth, Frankenmuth, MI. 1954.
5.75 - W - C.   Repainted #180

180. Frankenmuth, Frankenmuth, MI. 1954.
5.75 - Bk, Bl, Cr - C.

181. Frankenmuth, Frankenmuth, MI. 1954.
6 - Bk, Bl, Cr - C.

182. Frankenmuth, Frankenmuth, MI. 1954.
6 - Bk, Bl, Cr - C.

183. Frankenmuth, Frankenmuth, MI. 1951.
10 - Bk, Y, F, W - C.

184. Frankenmuth, Frankenmuth, MI. 1951.
10 - Bk, Y, F, W - C.

185. Frankenmuth, Frankenmuth, MI. 1951.
10 - Bk, Y, F, W - C.

186. Frankenmuth, Frankenmuth, MI. 1951.
10 - Bk, Y, F, W - C.

187. Frankenmuth, Buffalo, NY. 1953.
12.5 - R, W - C.

BEER STATUES

188. Fremlins, London, GB. 1955.
5.5 - Gy, R, W, Gd - P.   Rare

189. Gettelman, Milwaukee, WI. 1956.
14.5 - Bn, F, Cr, Gd - Co.

190. Gettelman, Milwaukee, WI. 1955.
14.5 - Bn, F, Cr, Gd - Co.

190a. Gettelman, Milwaukee, WI. 1953.
7 - Bk, F, W, R - W.

191. Gibbons, Wilkes-Barre, PA. 1960.
11- Bn, Bk, W, R - C.

192. Gibbons, Wilkes-Barre, PA. 1960.
9 - Bn, R, Bl, W - C.

193. Gibbons, Wilkes-Barre, PA. 1945.
8.5 - W, Gn, R, T - C.

194. Gluek's, Minneapolis, MN. 1959.
9.5 - R, Bk, F, W - C.

195. Goebel, Detroit, MI. 1953.
10.5 - Gn, Y, R, W - C.

196. Goebel, Detroit, MI. 1953.
10.5 - Gn, Y, R, W - C.

197. Goebel, Detroit, MI. 1953.
6 - Gn, Y, R, W - C.

198. Goebel, Detroit, MI. 1953.
6 - Gn, Y, R, W - C.   Rare

199. Gold Bond, Cleveland, OH. 1952.
13.5 - Bl, W, Gd, F - C.   Rare

200. Grand Prize, Houston, TX. 1954.
10 - Bn, Cr, Bk, R - C.

201. Grizzly Bear, CN. 1985.
15 - Bl, R, W - P.

202. Grolsch, Enschede, DM. 1988.
10 - Gy, Bl, W, Bk - P.

203. Guiness, London, GB. 1950.
14 - Gn, R, Bk, W - C.

204. Guiness, London, GB. 1950.
14 - Gn, R, Bk, W - C.

205. Guiness, London, GB. 1950.
13 - Gn, R, Bk, W - C.

206. Guiness, London, GB. 1950.
7 - W, Bk, Bl, O - R.

207. Guiness, London, GB. 1955.
15 - Bk, O, Gr, W - Cr.

208. Gunther's, Baltimore, MD. 1957.
18.5 - W, Bk, R - C.   Rare

209. Gunther's, Baltimore, MD. 1957.
12 - W, R, Gn, Bk - R.   Rare

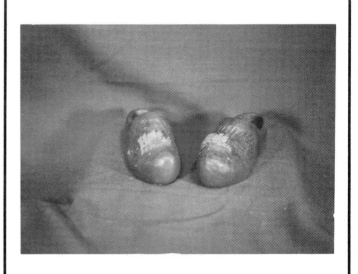

210. Hals, Baltimore, MD. 1952.
2.5 - Bn, Bl - C.

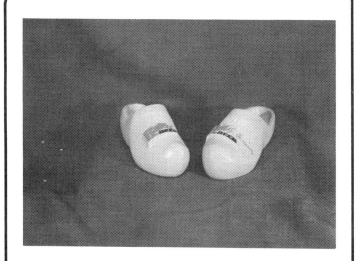

211. Hals, Baltimore, MD. 1952.
2.5 - Y, Bl, Bk - C.

212. Hamm's, St. Paul, MN. 1960.
16.5 - R, W, Bk, Bl - P.

213. Hamm's, St. Paul, MN. 1960.
16.5 - R, W, Bk, Bl - P.

214. Hamm's, St. Paul, MN. 1968.
15.5 - W, Bk, Bl, R - P.

215. Hamm's, St. Paul, MN. 1968.
15.5 - W, Bk, Bl, R - P.

216. Hamm's, St. Paul, MN. 1968.
15.5 - W, Bk, Bl, R - P.

217. Hamm's, St. Paul, MN. 1968.
    12 - Bk, W, R, Bl - F.

218. Hamm's, St. Paul, MN. 1973.
    11 - Bk, W, R - Cr.

219. Hamm's, St. Paul, MN. 1973.
    11 - Bk, W, R - Cr.

220. Hamm's, St. Paul, MN. 1959.
    12 - Bn, W, Gn, Bl - Cr.   Rare

221. Hamm's, St. Paul, MN. 1959.
    12 - Bk, W, Bl, Gn - Cr.

222. Hamm's, St. Paul, MN. 1959.
    12 - Bk, W, Bl, Gn - Cr.

223. Hamm's, St. Paul, MN. 1973.
10.8 - Bk, W, Bl, R - Cr.

224. Hamm's, St. Paul, MN. 1973.
10.8 - Bk, W, Bl, R - Cr.

225. Hamm's, St. Paul, MN. 1975.
20.5 - Bk, W, R - F.

226. Hamm's, St. Paul, MN. 1973.
11 - Bk, W, R - Cr.

227. Hampden, Willimansett, MA. 1947.
15 - Bn, W, Bk - C.

228. Hanley, Providence, RI. 1955.
12.5 - F, Bl, W - C.

229. Hanley's, Providence, RI. 1953.
9.5 - Gy, W, Bk - C.

230. Hanley's, Providence, RI. 1953.
9.5 - Gy, W, Bk - C.

231. Hanley's, Providence, RI. 1953.
9.5 - W, R, Y, Bk - Cl.

232. Hanley's, Providence, RI. 1953.
9.5 - W, Bl, Bk - Cl.

233. Hanley's, Providence, RI. 1953.
9.5 - W, R, Gn, Bk - Cl.

234. Hazelton, Hazelton, PA. 1948.
12 - W, Y, R, Bk - R.   Rare

235. Heidelberg, Tacoma, WA. 1958.
    6 - Gd, R - C.

236. Heidelberg, Tacoma, WA. 1958.
    6 - Gd, Gn - C.

237. Heidelberg, Tacoma, WA. 1958.
    9 - Gd, Bn - C.

238. Heidelberg, Tacoma, WA. 1958.
    9 - W, Bl, F, R - C.

239. Heidelberg, Tacoma, WA. 1958.
    9 - W, Bl, F, R - C.

240. Heidelberg, Tacoma, WA. 1958.
    8.5 - Cr, Bn, R, Bl - C.

BEER STATUES

241. Heidelberg, Tacoma, WA. 1958.
8.5 - Cr, Bn, R, Bl - C.

242. Heidelberg, Tacoma, WA. 1948.
13 - Cr, Bn, R, Bl - C.

243. Heidelberg, Tacoma, WA. 1948.
13.3 - Cr, Bn, R, Bl - C.

244. Heidelberg, Tacoma, WA. 1958.
9 - Bn, Cr, Gd, Bl - C.

245. Heidelberg, Tacoma, WA. 1958.
9 - Bn, Cr, Gd, Bl - CM. Lights

245a. Heidelberg, Belleville, IL. 1970.
8 - Gd, W, Wd - MW.

246. Heileman, LaCrosse, WI. 1970.
    19 - Wd - W.   Rare

247. Heineken, Amsterdam, HD. 1975.
    14 - Bn, Bk, R, W - C.

248. Heineken, Amsterdam, HD. 1962.
    19. 8 - Gn, Bn, Bk, R - C.

249. Heineken, Amsterdam, HD. 1975.
    20 - Gn, Bn, Bk, R - R.

250. Heineken, Amsterdam, HD. 1975.
    14 - Bn, Bk, R, W - C.

251. Heineken, Amsterdam, HD. 1975.
    14 - Gn, Bn, Bk, R - C.

BEER STATUES

252. Heineken, Amsterdam, HD. 1975.
    4 - Y, Bk, R - W.

253. Heineken, Amsterdam, HD. 1975.
    4 - Y, Bk, R - W.

254. Heineken, Amsterdam, HD. 1975.
    21 - Gd, Bn, Bk, W - FP.

255. Hensler, Newark, NJ. 1951.
    6 - Bk, Y, Bl, R - R.   Rare

256. Hoff Brau, Ft. Wayne, IN. 1956.
    10 - Cr, Bk, R - C.

257. Holland, Wylre, HD. 1985.
    13 - Gn, W, Bl, R - W.

258. Horlacher, Allentown, PA. 1960.
    10.5 - Bk, Cr, W, R - F. Rare

259. Hudepohl, Cincinnati, OH. 1953.
    9 - W, Bl, R - C.

260. Hudepohl, Cincinnati, OH. 1953.
    9 - W, Bl, R - C.

261. Hudepohl, Cincinnati, OH. 1968.
    16 - Cr, Bn, Bl, W - C.

262. Hudepohl, Cincinnati, OH. 1968.
    16 - Cr, Bn, Bl, W - C.

263. Hudepohl, Cincinnati, OH. 1955.
    12.5 - Bl, W, Y, R - C.

267. (Imperial) Ajax, Indianapolis, IN. 1955.
   15 - Gd, W, R - C.   Rare

268. Iron City, Pittsburg, PA. 1958.
   10 - Cr, R, Bk - C.

269. Iron City, Pittsburg, PA. 1958.
   10 - Bn, Cr, R, Bk - C.   Repainted #268

270. Iron City, Pittsburg, PA. 1958.
   10 - Cr, R, W, Bk - C.

271. Iroquois, Buffalo, NY. 1956.
   6 - Cr, Gd, Bn, Bl - R.

272. Iroquois, Buffalo, NY. 1956.
   6 - Br - M.

273. Iroquois, Buffalo, NY. 1956.
6 - Gd, R - M.

274. Jax, New Orleans, LA. 1946.
9 - Gd, Gn - C.   Rare

275. Jax, New Orleans, LA. 1958.
16.5 - W, F, Bl, R - P.

276. Kamm's, Mishawaka, IN. 1958.
11 - Cr, F, Bn, R - C.

277. King Kole, Cleveland, OH. 1963.
6.5 - W, F, R, Gd - C.

278. Kirin, Tokyo, JA. 1965.
10 - R, Bl, W - P.   Lights

279. Koch's, Dunkirk, NY. 1960.
8 - Br, R, W - C.

280. Krantz, Erie, PA. 1940.
12 - Bn, Gy, Gn, Cr - C.   Rare

281. Kruger, Newark, NJ. 1936.
7 - Bn, Si - R.

281a. Kruger, Newark, NJ. 1936.
7 - Si - M.   Repainted #281

281b. Krueger, Newark, NJ. 1953.
7 - Si - M.

282. Kuebler, Easton, PA. 1960.
10.5 - W, Y, Gn - C.   Rare

283. Labatt, Toronto, CN. 1972.
14 - Bl, W, R, F - Cr.

284. Labatt, Toronto, CN. 1972.
14 - Gn, R, F, W - Cr.

285. Labatt's, Toronto, CN. 1967.
9.5 - R, Bn, F, W - P.

286. Labatt's, Toronto, CN. 1967.
9 - R, Bn, F, W - P.

287. Labatt's, Toronto, CN. 1967.
10 - R, Bn, F, W - P.

288. Labatt's, Toronto, CN. 1967.
10 - R, Bn, F, W - P.

289. Leinenkugel's, Chippewa Falls, WI. 1988.
12.5 - F, Gn, W - C.

290. Leinenkugel's, Chippewa Falls, WI. 1959.
14 - F, Gn, W - P.

291. Lion, New York, NY. 1950.
8.5 - Bn, Bk, W - C.

292. Lion, New York, NY. 1950.
8.5 - Bn, Cr, Bk, R - C.

293. Lion, New York, NY. 1939.
16 - Bl, Cr, Gn - C.   Rare

294. Lion, New York, NY. 1945.
6 - Wd, Gd - WM.

295. Lone Star, San Antonio, TX. 1958.
    8 - Bn, Bk, R, W - C.

296. Lone Star. 1958.
    7.5 - T - C.   Novelty

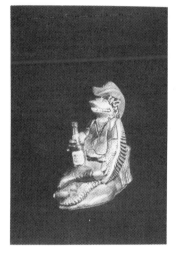

297. Lone Star. 1958.
    7.5 - Sl, Bl, Gn, G - C.   Novelty

298. Lone Star. 1958.
    7.5 - R, Gd, O, W - C.   Novelty

299. Lone Star. 1958.
    8 - Bn - C.   Novelty

300. Lone Star. 1958.
    8 - Gy - C.   Novelty

301. Lone Star, San Antonio, TX. 1958.
12 - Gy, Gn - C.

302. Lone Star, San Antonio, TX. 1958.
12 - Gy, Gn, Bn - C.

303. Lone Star, San Antonio, TX. 1958.
12 - Bn - C.

304. Lone Star. 1958.
7.5 - Gd, T, Cr - C.   Novelty

305. Lone Star, San Antonio, TX. 1958.
10 - Gy, Gn, R - C.

306. Lone Star. 1958.
7.5 - Gy, T, Cr, R - C.   Novelty

307. Lone Star. 1958.
    7.5 - Gy, Bn, Gr, R - C. Novelty

308. Lowenbrau, Munich, GY. 1975.
    14 - Bn, Gy - Pa.

309. Lowenbrau, Munich, GY. 1975.
    12.5 - Bn, Gy - P.

310. Lowenbrau, Munich, GY. 1975.
    13.5 - Bn, Gy, Cr, Bl - P.

311. Lowenbrau, Munich, GY. 1975.
    13 - Bn, Si, R, Bk - P.

312. Lowenbrau, Munich, GY. 1975.
    13 - Bn, R, W - C.

313. Lowenbrau, Munich, GY. 1975.
18 - Gd, Bk - C.

314. Lowenbrau, Munich, GY. 1975.
19 - Gd, Bk, W - C.   Lights

315. Lucky Lager, San Francisco, CA. 1950.
11.5 - Y, Gn, M - C.

316. Lucky Lager, San Francisco, CA. 1950.
11 - Y, Gn, M - C.

317. Lucky Lager, San Francisco, CA. 1950.
11 - W, Gn, Bn, Bl - C.

318. M & B, Burton-on-Trent, GB. 1947.
9 - T, Gn - R.   Rare

319. McEwan's, New Castle, SC. 1965.
10 - Bk, R, Y, Bl - R.

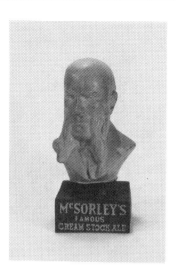

320. McSorley's, New York, NY. 1953.
9 - Cr, Bk, W - R.   Rare

321. Metz, Omaha, NE. 1956.
6.5 - T, Bk, R, W - Cr.

322. Metz, Omaha, NE. 1956.
6.5 - T - Cr.

323. Metz, Omaha, NE. 1956.
8 - Bn, Bk, R - C.

324. Metz, Omaha, NE. 1956.
12.5 - Bn, Bk, R - C.

325. Michelob, St. Louis, MO. 1966.
24 - W, Bk - P.   Lights

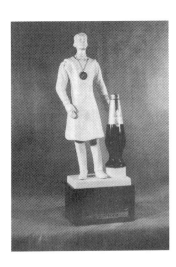

326. Michelob, St. Louis, MO. 1966.
24 - W, Bn - PW.   Lights

327. Michelob, St. Louis, MO. 1966.
15 - Bn, W, R - P.

328. Michelob, St. Louis, MO. 1966.
27 - W, Bn - PW.

329. Miller, Milwaukee, WI. 1951.
14.8 - R, F, Cr, Bn - C.

330. Miller, Milwaukee, WI. 1951.
14.8 - Cr, Bl, R, Bk - C.   Rare - Prototype

331. Miller, Milwaukee, WI. 1951.
14.8 - R, F, Cr, Bn - C.

332. Miller, Milwaukee, WI. 1951.
14 - R, F, Cr, Bn - C.

333. Miller, Milwaukee, WI. 1951.
6 - Gd, R - P.

334. Miller, Milwaukee, WI. 1951.
6 - R, F, Cr, Bn - P.

335. Miller, Milwaukee, WI. 1951.
6 - Gd, R - P.

336. Miller, Milwaukee, WI. 1951.
6 - Gd, R - P.

337. Miller, Milwaukee, WI. 1960.
6.5 - W, Bl, Y, Bk - P.

337a. Miller, Milwaukee, WI. 1951.
6 - Gd - P.

338. Mug Ale, Akron, OH. 1953.
6.75 - Bn, W - C.

339. Mug Ale, Akron, OH. 1953.
6.75 - Bn, W, R - C.   Repainted #338

No Picture Available

Almost Identical to #338

340. Mug Ale, Akron, OH. 1953.
6.75 - Bn, W - C.

341. Mustang, Pittsburg, PA. 1972.
10.5 - Gd, Bk - WP.

COLOR SECTION

258. *This statue was issued in 1960 by the Horlacher Brewing Company of Allentown, PA. It promotes Horlacher brand beer and stands about 10.5 inches tall.*

515. *This statue was issued in 1963 by the Jones Brewing Company of Smithton, PA. It promotes Stoney's brand beer and stands about 9.5 inches tall.*

151. This statue was issued in 1953 by the Falls City Brewing Company of Louisville, KY. It promotes Falls City brand beer and stands about 8.5 inches tall.

344. This statue was issued in 1953 by the National Brewing Company of Baltimore, MD. It promotes National Bohemian brand beer and stands about 7 inches tall.

255. This statue was issued in 1951 by the Hensler Brewing Company of Newark, NJ. It promotes Hensler brand beer and stands about 6 inches tall.

481. This statue was issued in 1960 by the Latrobe Brewing Company of Latrobe, PA. It promotes Rolling Rock brand beer and stands about 14 inches tall.

1. This statue was issued in 1953 by the Arizona Brewing Company of Phoenix, AZ. It promotes A-1 brand beer and stands about 11 inches tall.

506. This statue was issued in 1955 by the Sebewaing Brewing Company of Philadelphia, PA. It promotes Sebewaing brand beer and stands about 4 inches tall.

82. *This statue was issued in 1951 by the Acme Brewing Company of San Francisco, CA. It promotes Bull Dog brand beer and stands about 8 inches tall.*

274. *This statue was issued in 1946 by the Jackson Brewing Company of New Orleans, LA. It promotes Jax brand beer and stands about 9 inches tall.*

152. *This statue was issued in 1951 by the Falls City Brewing Company of Louisville, KY. It promotes Falls City brand beer and stands about 8.5 inches tall.*

237. *This statue was issued in 1958 by the Columbia Brewing Company of Tacoma, WA. It promotes Heidelberg brand beer and stands about 9 inches tall.*

134. *This statue was issued in 1965 by the DuBois Brewing Company of DuBois, PA. It promotes DuBois brand beer and stands about 12 inches tall.*

397. *This statue was issued in 1939 by the Enterprise Brewing Company of Fall River, MA. It promotes Old Tap brand beer and stands about 9 inches tall.*

147. *This statue was issued in 1953 by the Esslinger Brewing Company of Philadelphia, PA. It promotes Esslinger brand beer and stands about 19 inches tall.*

148. *This statue was issued in 1976 by the Falls City Brewing Company of Louisville, KY. It promotes Falls City brand beer and stands about 11 inches tall.*

199. *This statue was issued in 1952 by the Cleveland-Sandusky Brewing Company of Cleveland, OH. It promotes Gold Bond brand beer and stands about 13.5 inches tall.*

479. *This statue was issued in 1960 by the Latrobe Brewing Company of Latrobe, PA. It promotes Rolling Rock brand beer and stands about 14 inches tall.*

65. This statue was issued in 1959 by the Bosch Brewing Company of Houghton, MI. It promotes Bosch brand beer and stands about 10 inches tall.

66. This statue was issued in 1959 by the Bosch Brewing Company of Houghton, MI. It promotes Bosch brand beer and stands about 10 inches tall.

436. This statue was issued in 1952 by the Pfeiffer Brewing Company of Detroit, MI. It promotes Pfeiffer's brand beer and stands about 15 inches tall.

466. This statue was issued in 1956 by the Red Top Brewing Company of Cincinnati, OH. It promotes Redtop brand beer and stands about 13 inches tall.

71. *This statue was issued in 1934 by the Peter Breidt Brewing Company of Elizabeth, NJ. It's promotes Breidt's brand beer and stands about 17.5 inches tall.*

234. *This statue was issued in 1948 by the Hazleton-Lion Brewing Company of Hazleton, PA. It promotes Hazleton brand beer and stands about 12 inches tall.*

282. *This statue was issued in 1960 by the Kuebler Brewing Company of Easton, PA. It promotes Kuebler brand beer and stands about 10.5 inches tall.*

455. *This statue was issued in 1936 by the Poth Brewing Company of Philadelphia, PA. It promotes Poth brand beer and stands about 18 inches tall.*

107. *This statue was issued in 1940 by the Delta Brewing Company of Escanaba, MI. It promotes Delta brand beer and stands about 8.5 inches tall.*

156. *This statue was issued in 1954 by the Falstaff Brewing Company of St. Louis, MO. It promotes Falstaff brand beer and stands about 16.5 inches tall.*

246. *This statue was issued in 1970 by the Heileman Brewing Company of LaCrosse, WI. It promotes Heileman brand beer and stands about 19 inches tall.*

504. *This statue was issued in 1935 by the Schott Brewing Company of Highland, IL. It promotes Schott brand beer and stands about 11 inches tall.*

108. *This statue was issued in 1953 by the Diplomat Brewing Company of New Brittain, CT. It promotes Diplomat brand beer and stands about 14 inches tall.*

169. *This statue was issued in 1953 by the Fehr's Brewing Company of Cincinnati, OH. It promotes Fehr's brand beer and stands about 15.5 inches tall.*

503. *This statue was issued in 1952 by the Schoenling Brewing Company of Cincinnati, OH. It promotes Schoenling brand beer and stands about 16 inches tall.*

546. *This statue was issued in 1969 by the Fessenmeir Brewing Company of Huntington, WV. It promotes West Virginia brand beer and stands 15 inches tall.*

5. This statue was issued in 1955 by the Fox DeLuxe Brewing Company of Grand Rapids, MI. It promotes Alpine brand beer and stands about 11 inches tall.

68. This statue was issued in 1938 by the Boston Beer Brewing Company of Boston, MA. It promotes Boston Light Ale and stands about 22 inches tall.

422. This statue was issued in 1952 by the Fox DeLuxe Brewing Company of Grand Rapids, MI. It promotes Patrick Henry brand beer and stands about 10.8 inches tall.

468. This statue was issued in 1958 by the American Brewing Company of New Orleans, LA. It promotes Regal brand beer and stands about 10 inches tall.

102. This statue was issued in 1940 by the Cooper Brewing Company of Philadelphia, PA. It promotes Cooper's brand beer and stands about 15 inches tall.

175. This statue was issued in 1949 by the Fox DeLuxe Brewing Company of Grand Rapids, MI. It promotes Fox DeLuxe brand beer and stands about 16 inches tall.

209. This statue was issued in 1957 by the Gunther Brewing Company of Baltimore, MD. It promotes Gunther's brand beer and stands about 12 inches tall.

544. This statue was issued in 1969 by the Little Switzerland Brewing Company of Huntington, W.V. It promotes West Virginia brand beer and stands about 10.5 inches tall.

69. *This statue was issued in 1955 by the Boswell Brewing Company of Quebec, CN. It promotes Boswell brand beer and stands about 15 inches tall.*

168. *This statue was issued in 1953 by the Fehr's Brewing Company of Cincinnati, OH. It promotes Fehr's brand beer and stands about 15.5 inches tall.*

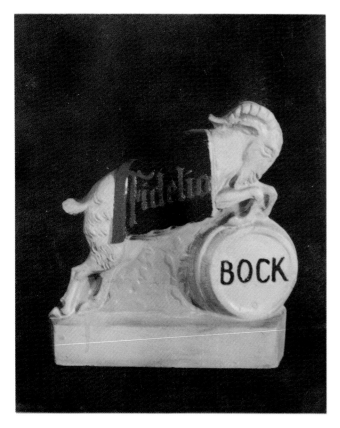

171. *This statue was issued in 1940 by the Fidelio Brewing Company of New York, NY. It promotes Fidelio brand beer and stands about 9.5 inches tall.*

267. *This statue was issued in 1955 by the Ajax Brewing Company of Indianapolis, IN. It promotes Imperial brand beer and stands about 15 inches tall.*

342. My, Omaha, NE. 1959.
6.5 - Bn, Bk, R - Cr.

344. National Bohemian, Baltimore, MD. 1953.
7 - W, R, Gn, F - Cr.

345. National Bohemian, Baltimore, MD. 1953.
7 - W, R, Gn, F - Cr.

346. National Bohemian, Baltimore, MD. 1953.
6 - Si - M.

347. National Bohemian, Baltimore, MD. 1953.
8 - R, Bk, F, W - PR.

348. National Bohemian, Baltimore, MD. 1953.
8 - R, Bk, F, W - WR.

349. National Bohemian, Baltimore, MD. 1953.
10 - R, Bk, F, W - PR.

350. National Bohemian, Detroit, MI. 1953.
6 - Bn, Gy, R, W - C.   Rare

351. National Bohemian, Baltimore, MD. 1953.
6 - Bn, Bk, Gy, F - C.

352. National Bohemian, Baltimore, MD. 1953.
10 - R, Bk, F, W - P.

353. Neuweiler, Allentown, PA. 1955.
12 - Y, Bk, R, W - P.   Rare

354. Neuweiler, Allentown, PA. 1957.
8 - Bn, Gy, Y, W - C.

355. Oertels, Louisville, KY. 1954.
14.3 - W, Bl, R, Bk - C.

356. Oertels, Louisville, KY. 1954.
16.3 - W, Bk, R, Gd - C.   Reproduction

357. Oertels, Louisville, KY. 1954.
14.8 - Bn, Gy, Bk, W - C. Reproduction

358. Oertels, Louisville, KY. 1954.
13 - W, Gy, R, Bk - C.

359. Oertels, Louisville, KY. 1954.
12.5 - O, T, Bk - C.

360. Oertels, Louisville, KY. 1954.
7.75 - W, Bk, R - C.   Reproduction

361. Oertels, Louisville, KY. 1954.
    9.75 - F, Bn, W, Bk - C. Reproduction

362. Oertels, Louisville, KY. 1954.
    9 - Cl - G.

363. Oertels, Louisville, KY. 1954.
    9 - F, Bn, W, R - C.   Reproduction

364. Oertels, Louisville, KY. 1954.
    9 - F, Bn, W, R - C.   Reproduction

365. Oertels, Louisville, KY. 1954.
    14 - F, Bn, W, R - C.   Reproduction

366. Old Appleton. 1950.
    12 - Bn, W, Gy - C.   Rare

367. Old Brew, Chicago, IL. 1945.
12 - Bn, Gy, R, W - C.   Rare

368. Old Dutch, Findlay, OH. 1952.
12 - Gd - R.

369. Old Dutch, Findlay, OH. 1952.
12 - Bn - R.

370. Old Dutch, Findlay, OH. 1952.
12 - Gy, R, F, Y - R.

371. Old Export, Cumberland, MD. 1960.
14 - Gn, Bk, Bn, Sl - C.   Rare

372. Old Export, Cumberland, MD. 1960.
14 - Gn, Cr, W - C.   Rare

373. Old Export, Cumberland, MD. 1960.
7.5 - Cr, Y, R, Bk - C.

374. Old German, Cumberland, MD. 1948.
5.5 - Bn, W, Bk - Cr.

375. Old German, Cumberland, MD. 1948.
6 - Cr, Bn, R, W - C.   Rare

376. Old German, Cumberland, MD. 1965.
12 - W, R, Gn, Bk - P.

377. Old German, Cumberland, MD. 1969.
13.3 - Bn, W, R, Bl - F.

378. Old German, Cumberland, MD. 1952.
14 - Gn, Cr, R, Bk - C.   Rare

379. Old German, Cumberland, MD. 1969.
12 - Bn, W, R, Bl - C.

380. Old German, Cumberland, MD. 1969.
14 - Gn, Cr, R, Bk - C.

380a. Old Imperial, Green Bay, WI. 1954.
12.5 - Gn, R, F - C.

380b. Old Imperial, Green Bay, WI. 1954.
12 - Gn, R, F - C.

380c. Old Imperial, Green Bay, WI. 1954.
12 - Gn, R, F - C.

381. Old Reading, Reading, PA. 1957.
12 - Bn, Cr, Gn, R - C.

382. Old Reading, Reading, PA. 1957.
12.5 - Bn, Cr, Gn, R - C.

383. Old Reading, Reading, PA. 1957.
12 - Bn, Cr, Gn, R - C.   Rare

384. Old Reading, Reading, PA. 1957.
12 - Bk, Y, Bn, F - C.

385. Old Reading, Reading, PA. 1957.
23.5 - Bn, Gn, Cr, R - C. Rare/Lights

386. Old Reading, Reading, PA. 1957.
3 - R, Bl, F, Y - C.

387. Old Reading, Reading, PA. 1957.
2.75 - Gd - M.

388. Old Reading, Reading, PA. 1957.
12 - Bk, Y, Bn, F - C.

389. Old Reading, Reading, PA. 1956.
16.5 - R, Gn, Bn, Si - C.   Rare/Prototype

390. Old Shay, Pittsburg, PA. 1950.
11.5 - W, R, Bk - C.

391. Old Shay, Pittsburg, PA. 1950.
11.5 - W, R, Bk - CR.

392. Old Shay, Pittsburg, PA. 1950.
11.5 - W, R, Bl, Bk - C.

393. Old Shay, Pittsburg, PA. 1950.
19 - W, R, Bk - CR.   Rare/Lights

394. Old Style, LaCrosse, WI. 1955.
7.5 - Gd - M.

395. Old Style, LaCrosse, WI. 1955.
24 - R, Bl, Bk, Gd - C.

396. Old Style, LaCrosse, WI. 1953.
8 - Bn, Gn, Bk, Gd - C.   Rare

397. Old Tap, Fall River, MA. 1939.
9 - Bl, O, F, Bk - C.   Rare

398. Old Timer, Cleveland, MD. 1961.
6 - Bn, R, Bl, F - C.

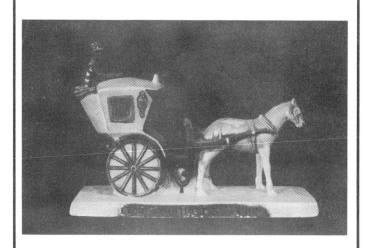

399. Old Timers, Cumberland, MD. 1961.
12 - Cr, Bk, R, Bn - C.

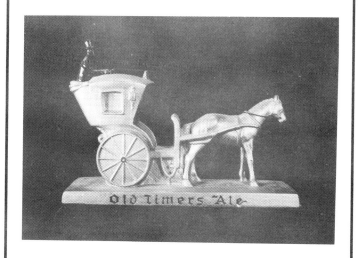

400. Old Timers, Cleveland, OH. 1961.
   12 - Gd, Bk, R - C.

401. Old Timers, Cleveland, OH. 1961.
   14 - Cr, R - C.

402. Old Vienna, Cincinnati, OH. 1960.
   6.25 - Cr - C.

403. Old Vienna, Cincinnati, OH. 1960.
   6.25 - Cr, Br, Gn- C.

404. P.O.C., Cleveland, OH. 1955.
   10.3 - Gn, W, Gy, Bn - C.

405. Pabst, Milwaukee, WI. 1957.
   15 - Cr, Bl, W - C.

406. Pabst, Milwaukee, WI. 1957.
10 - W, Bl, F, R - C.

407. Pabst, Milwaukee, WI. 1941.
10.3 - Y, Bn, Bl, F - C.   Rare

408. Pabst, Milwaukee, WI. 1958.
11 - W, Si, Bl, R - M.

409. Pabst, Milwaukee, WI. 1958.
11 - W, Si, Bl, R - M.

410. Pabst, Milwaukee, WI. 1958.
18 - W, Gd, Bn, Y - M.   Lights

411. Pabst, Milwaukee, WI. 1958.
14 - Gd, R, W, Bl - M.

412. Pabst, Milwaukee, WI. 1958.
    14 - Gd, R, W, Bl - M.

413. Pabst, Milwaukee, WI. 1958.
    11 - R, Bk, W, Gd - MP.

414. Pabst, Milwaukee, WI. 1958.
    11 - Bk, Bn, W, R - M.   Repainted #415

415. Pabst, Milwaukee, WI. 1958.
    11 - Bn, R, W, Bl - M.

416. Pabst, Milwaukee, WI. 1958.
    11 - Bn, R, W, Bl - M.

417. Pabst, Milwaukee, WI. 1957.
    7 - Bk, F, R, W - M.

418. Pabst. 1958.
    10 - Bn, W, Gn, F - C.   Fake (see #268)

419. Pabst, Milwaukee, WI. 1958.
    18 - W, Gd, Bn, Y - M.   Lights

420. Pabst, Milwaukee, WI. 1958.
    11 - W, Si, Bl, R - M.

421. Pabst, Milwaukee, WI. 1958.
    14 - Gd, R, W, Bl - M.

422. Patrick Henry, Grand Rapids, MI. 1952.
    10.8 - W, R, Bk, Gn - C.   Rare

423. Patrick Henry, Grand Rapids, MI. 1954.
    10.8 - W, R, Bk, Gn - C.

424. Patrick Henry, Grand Rapids, MI. 1954.
    10.8 - W, R, Bk, Gn - C. Rare/Prototype

425. Pearl. 1980.
    7.5 - Gd, R, Bl - C.   Novelty

426. Pearl, Toronto, CN. 1950.
    6 - Bk, Gr, W - C.

427. Peter Hand's, Chicago, IL. 1953.
    8 - Bn, Bk, Bl, W - C.

428. Peter Hand's, Chicago, IL. 1953.
    12.5 - Bn, Bk, Bl, W - C.

429. Pfeiffer's, Detroit, MI. 1952.
    7.25 - Y, R, Bl, Cr - C.

430. Pfeiffer's, Detroit, MI. 1952.
7.25 - Y, R, Bl, Cr - C.

431. Pfeiffer's, Detroit, MI. 1952.
7.25 - Y, R, Bl, Cr - C.

432. Pfeiffer's, Detroit, MI. 1952.
10.8 - Y, R, Bl, Cr - C.

433. Pfeiffer's, Detroit, MI. 1952.
10.8 - Y, R, Bl, Cr - C.

434. Pfeiffer's, Detroit, MI. 1952.
14.5 - Y, R, Bl, Cr - C.

435. Pfeiffer's, Detroit, MI. 1952.
14.5 - Y, R, Bl, Cr - C.

436. Pfeiffer's, Detroit, MI. 1952.
15 - Y, R, Bl, Cr - C.

437. Pfeiffer's, Detroit, MI. 1952.
13 - Y, R, Bl, Cr - C.

438. Pfeiffer's, Detroit, MI. 1952.
13 - Y, R, Bl, Cr - C.   Rare

439. Pfeiffer's, Detroit, MI. 1952.
13 - Y, R, Bl, Cr - C.

440. Phoenix, Bay City, MI. 1950.
10 - Bn, Cr, R, Si - C.   Rare

441. Pick Flowers, London, GB. 1960.
15 - W, Bk, R, Gd - Cr.

442. Pickwick, Boston, MA. 1959.
13 - Bl, Gy, Bk, W - R.

443. Piels, Brooklyn, NY. 1963.
11.5 - Bl, W, R, O - R.

444. Piels, Brooklyn, NY. 1963.
11.5 - Bl, W, R, O - R.

445. Piels, Brooklyn, NY. 1963.
9.5 - Bl, R, Gn - M.

446. Piels, Brooklyn, NY. 1956.
8.25 - Gd, Bl, F, Y - M.

447. Piels, Brooklyn, NY. 1944.
4 - Bl, Y - R.   Rare

448. Piels, Brooklyn, NY. 1963.
6 - Bn, Y, R, Gn - R.

449. Piels, Brooklyn, NY. 1963.
6 - Bn, W, R, Cr - M.

450. Piels, Brooklyn, NY. 1963.
5.75 - Bn, R, Gn - R.

451. Piels, Brooklyn, NY. 1963.
6 - Cr, Gn, R - R.

452. Piels, Brooklyn, NY. 1973.
6 - Bn, Gd, W, R - P.

453. Pioneer, LaCrosse, WI. 1963.
9 - Bn, Gy, Bk, R - C.   Rare

454. Pitts, GB. 1950.
   14 - R, Bn, Cr, F - C.   Rare

455. Poth, Philadelphia, PA. 1936.
   18 - Bn, F, Gy, W - C.   Rare

456. Rainier, Seattle, WA. 1959.
   7.5 - W, R, Bl - C.   Rare

457. Rainier, Seattle, WA. 1955.
   15 - T, W, Si, R - C.

458. Rainier, Seattle, WA. 1955.
   15 - Bn, Cr, W, Gn - C.

459. Rainier, Seattle, WA. 1955.
   16 - W, F, Bk, R - R.

460. Rainier, Seattle, WA. 1955.
16 - W, F, Bk, R - F.

461. Rainier, Seattle, WA. 1955.
16 - Gd, R - C.

462. Rainier, Seattle, WA. 1956.
8 - Bn, Gd, R, W - C.

463. Rainier, Seattle, WA. 1956.
7 - W, B, R, Gn - C.

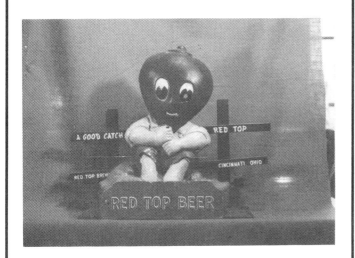

464. Red Top, Cincinnati, OH. 1956.
13 - Bl, R, W - RW.   Rare (as Beer)

465. Red Top, Cincinnati, OH. 1956.
13 - Bl, R, W - RW.

466. Red Top, Cincinnati, OH. 1956.
13 - Bl, R, Gn - C.

467. Regal, San Francisco, CA. 1956.
10 - Cr, Bl, R, Gd - C.

468. Regal, New Orleans, LA. 1958.
10 - Gn, W, Gy, Bn - C.   Rare

469. Renner, Ft. Wayne, IN. 1968.
7.5 - Gn, Cr, R, Y - C.   Rare

470. Renner, Ft. Wayne, IN. 1968.
14 - Bk, F, W, Gd - C.   Rare

471. Rheingold, New York, NY. 1972.
11.5 - W, R - F.

BEER STATUES

472. Rolling Rock, Latrobe, PA. 1960.
    11 - Bn, W, Gn, Bk - C.

473. Rolling Rock, Latrobe, PA. 1960.
    10.8 - Bn, Bl, W, Bk - C.

474. Rolling Rock, Latrobe, PA. 1960.
    11 - Bn, W, Gn, Bk - C.

475. Rolling Rock, Latrobe, PA. 1960.
    12 - Bn, M - F.

476. Rolling Rock, Latrobe, PA. 1960.
    14 - Bn, Gn, Bk - C.

477. Rolling Rock, Latrobe, PA. 1960.
    14 - W, Gn - C.

478. Rolling Rock, Latrobe, PA. 1960.
18 - W, R, Bk - C.

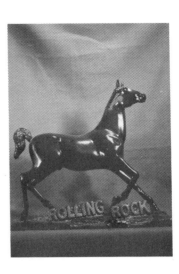

479. Rolling Rock, Latrobe, PA. 1960.
14 - Bn, Bk, Y - Pa.   Rare

480. Rolling Rock, Latrobe, PA. 1960.
19 - Bn, Bk, Cr - C.

481. Rolling Rock, Latrobe, PA. 1960.
14 - Gn, Gy, Gd, Bk - C. Rare - Color

482. Royal Bohemian, Duluth, MN. 1960.
14 - Bl, F, W - C.

483. Ruppert, New York, NY. 1940.
10 - W, R - C.

483a. Ruppert, New York, NY. 1940.
9 - Bn - C.

483b. Ruppert, New York, NY. 1940.
6 - Bn, Y, R, W - C.

484. Schell's, New Ulm, WI. 1960.
9 - Bn, Bk, R, W - C.

485. Schiltz, Milwaukee, WI. 1955.
26 - Bl, F, Gd, Gn - MP.

486. Schiltz, Milwaukee, WI. 1960.
20 - Gd - M.

487. Schiltz, Milwaukee, WI. 1960.
45 - Gd, Bl, R, W - P.

488. Schiltz, Milwaukee, WI. 1960.
12.5 - Gd, W - MP.

489. Schiltz, Milwaukee, WI. 1960.
5 - Gd, R, W - Cr.

490. Schiltz, Milwaukee, WI. 1955.
24 - Gd, Bl, R - M.

491. Schiltz. 1972.
9 - Bk, Br, Bl - Cr.   Fake

492. Schiltz, Milwaukee, WI. 1947.
36 - Gd - C.   Rare

493. Schmidt, St. Paul, MN. 1957.
3.5 - Gy, F, R, Y - P.

494. Schmidt's, Philadelphia, PA. 1955.
8.25 - Gd - M.

495. Schmidt's, Philadelphia, PA. 1955.
8.25 - Bn, Bk, W, R - M.

496. Schmidt's, Philadelphia, PA. 1955.
13 - Bn, Bk, W, R - C.

497. Schmidt's, Philadelphia, PA. 1955.
13 - Bn, Bk, W, R - M.

498. Schmidt's, Philadelphia, PA. 1955.
13 - Bn, Bk, W, R - R.

499. Schmidt's, Philadelphia, PA. 1963.
10 - Bn, W, Gd - C.

500. Schmidt's, Philadelphia, PA. 1960.
15 - W, O, R, Bk - F.

501. Schoenling, Cincinnati, OH. 1952.
13 - F, Bl, W - C.

502. Schoenling, Cincinnati, OH. 1952.
13 - F, Bl, W - C.

503. Schoenling, Cincinnati, OH. 1952.
16 - F, Bl, W - C.   Rare

504. Schott, Highland, IL. 1935.
11 - Gd - C.   Rare

505. Sebewaing, Sebewaing, MI. 1955.
4 - W, Bl, Bn, Y - C.   Rare

506. Sebewaing, Sebewaing, MI. 1955.
   4 - Bn, Gn, Bk - C.   Rare

507. Simon Pure, Buffalo, NY. 1957.
   9 - Bk, F, Bl, Y - C.

508. Standard, Rochester, NY. 1962.
   12.5 - Si, Gn, R - C.

509. Sterling, Evansville, IN. 1960.
   12 - Y, Cr, Si, F - C.

510. Sterling, Evansville, IN. 1960.
   9 - Y, W, R, Bl - C.

511. Sterling, Evansville, IN. 1960.
   11.5 - Si, Bl, W, R - C.

512. Sterling, Evansville, IN. 1960.
15 - Si, R, F, Bl - M.

513. Sterling, Evansville, IN. 1960.
15 - Y, Si, F, R - M.

514. Stoney's, Smithton, PA. 1963.
9.5 - Y, Bk, W - R.

515. Stoney's, Smithton, PA. 1963.
9.5 - Cr, Y, Bk, R - C.   Rare

516. Stoney's, Smithton, PA. 1963.
8.25 - Y, Bk, F - R.   Rare

517. Stoney's, Smithton, PA. 1972.
9.5 - R, Bk, F, W - C.

518. Strohs, Detroit, MI. 1970.
  10 - Gd, Bk - M.

519. Tadcaster, Worcester, MA. 1960.
  14 - Bk, F, W - C.   Rare

520. Tech, Pittsburg, PA. 1953.
  10 - Cr, Bn, Gn, R - C.   Repainted #521

521. Tech, Pittsburg, PA. 1953.
  10 - Cr, R, Bk - C.

522. Thousand Dollar, Milwaukee, WI. 1956.
  7 - Bk, W, R, F - W.

523. Tivoli, Denver, CO. 1955.
  16 - Bn, Cr, R, W - C.

524. Tivoli, Springfield, MA. 1897.
     8 - Wd, Si, R - WM.   Rare

525. Tivoli, Denver, CO. 1955.
     8 - T, Gy, R, W - C.

526. Toby, Toronto, CN. 1955.
     3 - Gn, Cr, R, F - C.

527. Topper, Rochester, NY. 1954.
     9 - Bk, W, R - C.

528. Tru Age, Scranton, PA. 1943.
     14.5 - Cr, Bk, F - C.   Rare

529. Utica Club, Utica, NY. 1948.
     7.5 - R, Bn, W, Gn - C.

530. Utica Club, Utica, NY. 1955.
10 - Y, F, W, Bl - C.

531. Utica Club, Utica, NY. 1955.
10 - Y, R, W, F - C.

532. Valley Forge, Philadelphia, PA. 1952.
9 - Gd, R, W - M.

533. Valley Forge, Philadelphia, PA. 1952.
14 - F, Bk, W - C.

534. Valley Forge, Philadelphia, PA. 1952.
14 - F, Bk, W - C.

535. Van Merritt, Burlington, WI. 1953.
14 - Y, W, Gy, Bk - C.   Rare

536. Van Merritt, Burlington, WI. 1953.
14 - Y, W, Gy, Bk - C.   Rare (Authentic?)

537. Watney's, London, GB. 1965.
12 - R, W, Wd, Bk - WCr.

538. Watney's, London, GB. 1965.
13 - Bk, Cl, Gr, W - P.

539. Wehle, West Haven, CT. 1939.
10.5 - W - C.   Rare

540. Wehle, West Haven, CT. 1939.
10 - W, Bk - C.   Rare

541. West Pennsylvania. 1960.
12 - Bn, Bk, Gn, W - Cr. Fake/Novelty

542. West Virginia, Huntington, WV. 1969.
10.5 - W, Bl, R - C.

543. West Virginia, Huntington, WV. 1969.
10.5 - W, Bl, R - C.

544. West Virginia, Huntington, WV. 1969.
10.5 - W, Bl, R - C.

545. West Virginia, Huntington, WV. 1969.
13 - W, Gy, R, Bk - C.

546. West Virginia, Huntington, WV. 1969.
15 - Bl, W, R, Gd - C.   Rare

546a. West Virginia, Huntington, WV. 1969.
8 - T, R, W - C.

547. Whitbread, London, GB. 1970.
9 - Bk, W, R - Cr.

548. Whitbread, London, GB. 1970.
14 - W, R, Bk, Gd - P.

549. Wielands, John; San Jose, CA. 1955.
9 - W, F - C.

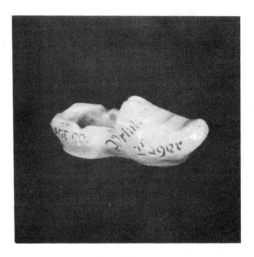

550. Wooden Shoe, Minster, OH. 1965.
2.5 - Cr, Bn - C.

551. Wunderbar, Minneapolis, MN. 1962.
16 - Cr, Bn, Gn, W - C.

552. Yankee, New York, NY. 1955.
12.5 - W, Bl, R - C.   Rare

553. Younger, Edinburgh, SC. 1970.
    8 - Bk, Y, R, W - R.

554. Yusay, Chicago, IL. 1951.
    9 - Bn, Bk, Bl, Y - C.

555. Yusay, Chicago, IL. 1951.
    9 - Cr, Gd - C.

556. Yusay, Chicago, IL. 1951.
    9 - Bn, Cr, R, Bk - C.   Rare

BEER SHELF SIGNS

801. Acme, Los Angeles, CA. 1940.
    3 - W, Bk, R - C.

802. American, Baltimore, MD. 1958.
    11 - Bn, W - Co.

803. American, Los Angeles, CA. 1958.
    3 - W, R, Gd, Bk - C.

804. Arrow, Baltimore, MD. 1953.
    3 - Cr, R, Bk - C.

805. Blitz, Portland, OR. 1951.
    3 - W, Bl, Bk, Bn - C.

806. Blue N' Gold, Santa Rosa, CA. 1955.
    5 - Y, Bl - C.

807. BOH, Fall River, MA. 1950.
8 - Y, R, Bl - C.

808. Brew 102, Los Angeles, CA. 1956.
5.5 - W, Bl, R, Bk - C.

809. Burkhardt's, Akron, OH. 1953.
3 - W, R, Bk - C.

810. Burkhardt's, Akron, OH. 1955.
7 - Gd - C.

811. Canadian Ace, Chicago, IL. 1955.
4 - W, R, Bk - C.

812. Champagne Velvet, Terre Haute, IN. 1952.
3 - W, Bk, R - C.

813. Champagne Velvet, Terre Haute, IN. 1952.
3 - W, Si - C.

814. Chief Oshkosh, Oshkosh, WI. 1957.
7 - T, W, R, Bl - C.

815. Columbia, Shenandoah, PA. 1961.
3 - W, R, Gr - C.

816. Columbia, Shenandoah, PA. 1948.
3 - W, R, Bl - C.

817. Drewrys, South Bend, IN. 1947.
3 - W, R, Bk - C.

818. Drewrys, South Bend, IN. 1947.
3 - R, W - C.

819. Drewrys, South Bend, IN. 1947.
3 - R, W - C.

820. DuBois Budweiser, DuBois, PA. 1968.
3 - Bn, Bk, Bl, R - C.

821. E & B, Detroit, MI. 1955.
7 - W, R, Bl - C.

822. E & B, Detroit, MI. 1955.
4 - W, R, Bl - C.

823. Esquire, Smithton, PA. 1973.
3 - W, R, Bk - C.

824. Falls City, Louisville, KY. 1940.
9.5 - R, Gn, Si - M.

825. Fehr's, Louisville, KY. 1953.
    3 - W, Bl, R - C.

826. Frankenmuth, Frankenmuth, MI. 1954.
    8 - Bn, Bl, Gd, W - C.

827. Goebel, Detroit, MI. 1952.
    5 - W, R, Bn, Bk - C.

828. Goebel, Detroit, MI. 1953.
    8 - W, R, Y, Bk - C.

829. Goebel, Detroit, MI. 1953.
    3 - W, R, Bk, Y - C.

830. Gretz, Philadelphia, PA. 1958.
    3 - R, W, Gy, Cr - C.

831. Gunther's, Baltimore, MD. 1957.
    3 - R, Bl, W - C.

832. Iron City, Pittsburg, PA. 1948.
    3 - Cr, R, W, Bk - C

833. Kamm's, Mishawaka, IN. 1950.
    3 - W, Gd, Bl, R - C.

834. Koehler's, Erie, PA. 1963.
    10 - Si, R - C.

835. Koehler's, Erie, PA. 1963.
    10 - W, R, Bl, Vi - C.

836. Koehler's, Erie, PA. 1963.
    10 - W, R, Bk, Gn - C.

837. Luxury, Los Angeles, CA. 1955.
3 - W, Bk, Gd, R - C.

838. National Bohemian, Baltimore, MD. 1953.
3 - W, R, F, Bk - C.

839. Old Dutch, Catasauqua, PA. 1952.
3 - W, R, Bk, Gd - C.

840. Old Export, Cumberland, MD. 1960.
3 - Gn, W, R, Bk - C.

841. Old Towne, Newark, OH. 1945.
10 - Bl, R, O, Y - C.

842. P.O.C., Cleveland, OH. 1952.
3 - W, R, Bl, Gn - C.

843. Pennsylvania Dutch, Lebanon, PA. 1957.
3 - W, Bk, R, Gn - C.

844. Silver Top, Pittsburg, PA. 1955.
3 - W, R, Bk, Y - C.

845. Standard, Rochester, NY. 1948.
3 - W, R, Bk - C.

846. Weber, Waukesha, WI. 1959.
5 - W, Bk, R, Gn - C.

847. Wooden Shoe, Minster, OH. 1950.
6 - W, F, R, Bl - C.

848. Wooden Shoe, Minster, OH. 1950.
6 - W, Bn, R, Bk - C.

PRICE GUIDE

PRICE GUIDE

ITEM NUMBER	PRICE RANGE	BREWERY	COMMENTS
1	450+	Arizona	Rare (Clock/Lights)
2	136-200	Acme	
3	136-200	Acme	
4	201-300	Acme	Rare
5	136-200	Fox Deluxe	
6	61-85	Altes	
7	86-135	Altes	
8	86-135	Altes	
9	35-60	Altes	
10	35-60	Altes	
11	35-60	Altes	
12	35-60	Altes	
13	86-135	American	
14	450+	Charters Valley	Rare
15	16-34	Ballantine	
16	201-300	General	Rare
17	61-85	Batholomay	Rare
18	86-135	Franklin Brewing	Rare
19	136-200	Dawes/National	
20	136-200	Dawes/National	
21	136-200	Dawes/National	
22	450+	Dawes/National	
23	136-200	Dawes/National	
24	136-200	Dawes/National	
25	450+	Dawes/National	
26	136-200	Dawes/National	
27	136-200	Dawes/National	
28	136-200	Dawes/National	
29	16-34	Koch	
30	16-34	Koch	
31	16-34	Koch	
32	86-135	Carling	
33	201-300	Blatz	
34	61-85	Blatz	Lights
35	61-85	Blatz	
36	61-85	Blatz	
37	61-85	Blatz	
39	136-200	Blatz	
40	86-135	Blatz	
41	35-60	Blatz	
42	35-60	Blatz	
43	16-34	Blatz	

PRICE GUIDE

ITEM NUMBER	PRICE RANGE	BREWERY	COMMENTS
44	16-34	Blatz	
45	16-34	Blatz	
46	61-85	Blatz	
47	35-60	Blatz	
48	35-60	Blatz	
49	35-60	Blatz	
50	35-60	Blatz	
51	35-60	Blatz	Lights
52	35-60	Blatz	
53	35-60	Blatz	
54	35-60	Blatz	
55	61-85	Blatz	
56	16-34	Blatz	
57	16-34	Blatz	
58	16-34	Blatz	
59	16-34	Blatz	
60	61-85	Blatz	Lights/Moves
61	35-60	Blatz	
62	35-60	Blatz	
63	35-60	Blatz	
64	86-135	Blitz	
65	301-450	Bosch	Rare
66	301-450	Bosch	
67	301-450	Bosch	
68	301-450	Boston Beer	Rare/Lights
69	136-200	Boswell	Rare
70	136-200	Carling	Rare
71	301-450	Peter Breidt	Rare
72	35-60	Bruck's	
73	61-85	Buckeye	
74	35-60	Anheuser-Busch	
75	35-60	Anheuser-Busch	
76	16-34		Novelty
77	16-34		Novelty
78	16-34	Anheuser-Busch	
79	136-200	Anheuser-Busch	
80	16-34		Novelty
81	136-200	Anheuser-Busch	
82	301-450	Acme	Rare
83	301-450	Acme	Rare
84	301-450	Acme	Rare
85	35-60	Burger	

PRICE GUIDE

ITEM NUMBER	PRICE RANGE	BREWERY	COMMENTS
86	61-85	Burger	Rare
87	61-85	Burger	Rare
88	35-60	Burger	
89	35-60	Burger	
90	136-200	San Francisco	
91	136-200	San Francisco	
92	86-135	San Francisco	Repainted #90
93	86-135	Burkhardt	
94	35-60	Burkhardt	Repainted #93
95	35-60	Anheuser-Busch	Lights
96	61-85	Brewery Unknown	Lights
97	35-60	Canadian Ace	
98	35-60	Carlsburg	
99	201-300	Oshkosh	
100	35-60	Oshkosh	
101	136-200	Cooper	
102	136-200	Cooper	
103	16-34		Fake
104	1-15		Novelty
105	301-450	Cleveland-Sandusky	Rare
106	86-135	Dakota	Rare
107	86-135	Delta Brewing Co.	Rare
108	86-135	Diplomat	Rare
109	61-85	Ind. Coope	
110	136-200	Drewrys	
111	136-200	Drewrys	
112	201-300	Drewrys	Lights
113	301-450	Drewrys	Rare
114	61-85	Drewrys	Lights
115	61-85	Drewrys	Lights
116	61-85	Drewrys	
117	61-85	Drewrys	
118	61-85	Drewrys	
119	61-85	Drewrys	
120	450+	Drewrys	Rare
121	16-34	Drewrys	
122	16-34	Drewrys	
123	16-34	Drewrys	
124	16-34	Drewrys	
125	16-34	Drewrys	
126	61-85	Drewrys	
127	16-34	Drewrys	

PRICE GUIDE

ITEM NUMBER	PRICE RANGE	BREWERY	COMMENTS
128	16-34	Drewrys	
129	16-34	Drewrys	
130	16-34	Drewrys	
131	35-60	Drewrys	
132	35-60	DuBois	
133	35-60	DuBois	
134	136-200	DuBois	Rare
135	86-135	Duquesne	
136	86-135	Duquesne	
137	35-60	Duquesne	
138	35-60	Duquesne	
139	86-135	General	
140	450+	C & J Michael	Rare
141	35-60	Standard	
142	35-60	Standard	
143	35-60	Standard	
144	35-60	Standard	
145	35-60	Standard	
146	301-450	Otto Erlanger	Rare
147	301-450	Esslinger	Rare
148	136-200	Falls City	
149	136-200	Falls City	
150	35-60	Falls City	
151	201-300	Falls City	Rare
152	136-200	Falls City	Rare
153	61-85	Falls City	
154	16-34	Falls City	
155	136-200	Falstaff	
156	61-85	Falstaff	
157	86-135	Falstaff	
158	86-135	Falstaff	
159	301-450	Falstaff	
160	301-450	Falstaff	
161	35-60	Falstaff	
162	61-85	Falstaff	
163	1-15	Falstaff	
164	16-34		Novelty
165	1-15		Novelty
166	1-15		Novelty
167	35-60	Falstaff	
168	86-135	Fehr's	
169	201-300	Fehr's	Rare

PRICE GUIDE

ITEM NUMBER	PRICE RANGE	BREWERY	COMMENTS
170	35-60	Fessenmeier	
171	201-300	Fidelio Brewing	Rare
172	35-60	Fitgers	
173	35-60	Fort Pitt	
174	201-300	Peter Fox	
175	201-300	Fox Deluxe	
176	201-300	Peter Fox	
177	61-85	Fox Head	
178	16-34	Fox Head	
179	16-34	Frankenmuth	Repainted #180
180	16-34	Frankenmuth	
181	16-34	Frankenmuth	
182	16-34	Frankenmuth	
183	61-85	Frankenmuth	
184	61-85	Frankenmuth	
185	61-85	Frankenmuth	
186	61-85	Frankenmuth	
187	86-135	International	
188	61-85	Whitbread	Rare
189	61-85	Miller	
190	61-85	Miller	
190a	16-34	Miller	
191	136-200	Lion Brewers	
192	86-135	Lion Brewers	
193	201-300	Lion Brewers	
194	61-85	Gluek's	
195	35-60	Goebel	
196	35-60	Goebel	
197	35-60	Goebel	
198	61-85	Goebel	Rare
199	450+	Cleveland-Sandusky	Rare
200	301-450	Gulf	
201	35-60	Brewery Unknown	
202	16-34	Grolsche	
203	86-135	Guiness	
204	86-135	Guiness	
205	86-135	Guiness	
206	61-85	Guiness	
207	86-135	Guiness	
208	301-450	Gunther	Rare
209	201-300	Gunther	Rare
210	16-34	Hals	

PRICE GUIDE

ITEM NUMBER	PRICE RANGE	BREWERY	COMMENTS
211	16-34	Hals	
212	16-34	Hamm's	
213	16-34	Hamm's	
214	16-34	Hamm's	
215	35-60	Hamm's	
216	16-34	Hamm's	
217	35-60	Hamm's	
218	16-34	Hamm's	
219	16-34	Hamm's	
220	301-450	Hamm's	Rare
221	201-300	Hamm's	
222	201-300	Hamm's	
223	16-34	Hamm's	
224	16-34	Hamm's	
225	35-60	Hamm's	
226	16-34	Hamm's	
227	86-135	Hampden	
228	61-85	Hanley	
229	136-200	Hanley	
230	136-200	Hanley	
231	201-300	Hanley	
232	201-300	Hanley	
233	201-300	Hanley	
234	301-450	Hazelton-Lion	Rare
235	86-135	Columbia Brew	
236	86-135	Columbia Brew	
237	136-200	Columbia Brew	
238	136-200	Columbia Brew	
239	136-200	Columbia Brew	
240	16-34	Columbia Brew	
241	16-34	Columbia Brew	
242	86-135	Columbia Brew	
243	86-135	Columbia Brew	
244	86-135	Columbia Brew	
245	86-135	Columbia Brew	Lights
245a	16-34	Carling	
246	136-200	Heileman	Rare
247	35-60	Heineken	
248	35-60	Heineken	
249	35-60	Heineken	
250	35-60	Heineken	
251	35-60	Heineken	

PRICE GUIDE

ITEM NUMBER	PRICE RANGE	BREWERY	COMMENTS
252	1-15	Heineken	
253	1-15	Heineken	
254	16-34	Heineken	
255	201-300	Hensler	Rare
256	86-135	Berghoff	
257	16-34	Royal Brand	
258	136-200	Horlacher	Rare
259	136-200	Hudepohl	
260	136-200	Hudepohl	
261	35-60	Hudepohl	
262	35-60	Hudepohl	
263	201-300	Hudepohl	
267	201-300	Ajax	Rare
268	61-85	Pittsburg	
269	35-60	Pittsburg	Repainted #268
270	61-85	Pittsburg	
271	61-85	Iroquois	
272	61-85	Iroquois	
273	61-85	Iroquois	
274	201-300	Jackson	Rare
275	86-135	Jackson	
276	86-135	Kamm's	
277	61-85	King's Brewery	
278	35-60	Kirin	Lights
279	35-60	Fred Koch	
280	450+	Erie	Rare
281	35-60	Krueger	
281a	35-60	Krueger	Repainted #281
281b	35-60	Krueger	
282	301-450	Kuebler	Rare
283	86-135	Labatt	
284	86-135	Labatt	
285	1-15	Labatt	
286	1-15	Labatt	
287	1-15	Labatt	
288	1-15	Labatt	
289	16-34	Leinenkugel	
290	61-85	Leinenkugel	
291	136-200	Lion	
292	136-200	Lion	
293	301-450	Lion	Rare
294	35-60	Lion	

PRICE GUIDE

ITEM NUMBER	PRICE RANGE	BREWERY	COMMENTS
295	35-60	Lone Star	
296	1-15		Novelty
297	1-15		Novelty
298	1-15		Novelty
299	1-15		Novelty
300	1-15		Novelty
301	86-135	Lone Star	
302	86-135	Lone Star	
303	86-135	Lone Star	
304	1-15		Novelty
305	86-135	Lone Star	
306	1-15		Novelty
307	1-15		Novelty
308	61-85	Lowenbrau	
309	61-85	Lowenbrau	
310	61-85	Lowenbrau	
311	35-60	Lowenbrau	
312	86-135	Lowenbrau	
313	35-60	Lowenbrau	
314	61-85	Lowenbrau	Lights
315	86-135	Lucky	
316	86-135	Lucky	
317	86-135	Lucky	
318	201-300	Bass (Anchor)	Rare
319	86-135	McEwan's	
320	136-200	Liebmann	Rare
321	16-34	Metz	
322	16-34	Metz	
323	35-60	Metz	
324	35-60	Metz	
325	86-135	Anheuser-Busch	Lights
326	86-135	Anheuser-Busch	Lights
327	61-85	Anheuser-Busch	
328	86-135	Anheuser-Busch	
329	86-135	Miller	
330	136-200	Miller	Rare/Prototype
331	35-60	Miller	
332	86-135	Miller	
333	16-34	Miller	
334	35-60	Miller	
335	16-34	Miller	
336	16-34	Miller	

PRICE GUIDE

ITEM NUMBER	PRICE RANGE	BREWERY	COMMENTS
337	16-34	Miller	
337a	16-34	Miller	
338	35-60	Burkhardt	
339	35-60	Burkhardt	Repainted #338
340	35-60	Burkhardt	
341	35-60	Pittsburg	
342	35-60	My	
344	136-200	National	
345	136-200	National	
346	61-85	National	
347	61-85	National	
348	61-85	National	
349	61-85	National	
350	136-200	National	Rare
351	136-200	National	
352	61-85	National	
353	61-85	Neuweiler	Rare
354	35-60	Neuweiler	
355	201-300	Oertel's	
356	86-135	Oertel's	Reproductions
357	136-200	Oertel's	Reproductions
358	201-300	Oertel's	
359	35-60	Oertel's	
360	16-34	Oertel's	Reproductions
361	35-60	Oertel's	Reproductions
362	61-85	Oertel's	
363	35-60	Oertel's	Reproductions
364	35-60	Oertel's	Reproductions
365	35-60	Oertel's	Reproductions
366	86-135	Brewery Unknown	Rare
367	450+	Garden City	Rare
368	86-135	Krantz	
369	86-135	Krantz	
370	86-135	Krantz	
371	136-200	Cumberland	Rare
372	136-200	Cumberland	Rare
373	16-34	Cumberland	
374	86-135	Queen City	
375	136-200	Queen City	Rare
376	61-85	Queen City	
377	61-85	Queen City	
378	201-300	Queen City	Rare

PRICE GUIDE

ITEM NUMBER	PRICE RANGE	BREWERY	COMMENTS
379	61-85	Queen City	
380	201-300	Queen City	
380a	201-300	Old Imperial	
380b	201-300	Old Imperial	
380c	201-300	Old Imperial	
381	86-135	Old Reading	
382	136-200	Old Reading	
383	201-300	Old Reading	Rare
384	136-200	Old Reading	
385	136-200	Old Reading	Rare/Lights
386	35-60	Old Reading	
387	35-60	Old Reading	
388	136-200	Old Reading	
389	136-200	Old Reading	Rare/Prototype
390	86-135	Fort Pitt	
391	86-135	Fort Pitt	
392	86-135	Fort Pitt	
393	86-135	Fort Pitt	Rare/Lights
394	35-60	Heileman	
395	450+	Heileman	
396	201-300	Heileman	Rare
397	201-300	Enterprise	Rare
398	136-200	West Bend Lithia	
399	136-200	Cleveland- Sandusky	
400	136-200	West Bend Lithia	
401	136-200	West Bend Lithia	
402	35-60	Old Vienna	
403	35-60	Old Vienna	
404	86-135	Pilsner	
405	136-200	Pabst	
406	61-85	Pabst	
407	201-300	Pabst	Rare
408	61-85	Pabst	
409	61-85	Pabst	
410	61-85	Pabst	Lights
411	61-85	Pabst	
412	61-85	Pabst	
413	35-60	Pabst	
414	35-60	Pabst	Repainted #415
415	61-85	Pabst	
416	61-85	Pabst	
417	16-34	Pabst	

PRICE GUIDE

ITEM NUMBER	PRICE RANGE	BREWERY	COMMENTS
418	35-60		Fake (see #268)
419	86-135	Pabst	Lights
420	86-135	Pabst	
421	61-85	Pabst	
422	450+	Fox Deluxe	
423	136-200	Fox Deluxe	Rare
424	86-135	Fox Deluxe	Rare/Prototype
425	1-15		Novelty
426	86-135	Black Horse	
427	35-60	Peter Hand	
428	35-60	Peter Hand	
429	16-34	Pfeiffer	
430	16-34	Pfeiffer	
431	16-34	Pfeiffer	
432	35-60	Pfeiffer	
433	35-60	Pfeiffer	
434	86-135	Pfeiffer	
435	86-135	Pfeiffer	
436	136-200	Pfeiffer	
437	86-135	Pfeiffer	
438	86-135	Pfeiffer	Rare
439	86-135	Pfeiffer	
440	450+	Phoenix	Rare
441	136-200	Whitbread	
442	86-135	Haffenreffer	
443	35-60	Piels Bros.	
444	35-60	Piels Bros.	
445	86-135	Piels Bros.	
446	35-60	Piels Bros.	
447	86-135	Piels Bros.	Rare
448	35-60	Piels Bros.	
449	35-60	Piels Bros.	
450	35-60	Piels Bros.	
451	35-60	Piels Bros.	
452	1-15	Piels Bros.	
453	201-300	Pioneer	Rare
454	450+	Brewery Unknown	Rare
455	450+	Poth Brewing Co.	Rare
456	201-300	Sicks Rainier	Rare
457	136-200	Sicks Rainier	
458	136-200	Sicks Rainier	
459	136-200	Sicks Rainier	

PRICE GUIDE

ITEM NUMBER	PRICE RANGE	BREWERY	COMMENTS
460	61-85	Sicks Rainier	
461	136-200	Sicks Rainier	
462	61-85	Sicks Rainier	
463	35-60	Sicks Rainier	
464	136-200	Red Top	
465	136-200	Red Top	
466	201-300	Red Top	Rare (as Beer)
467	86-135	Regal	
468	86-135	American	Rare
469	86-135	Renner	Rare
470	86-135	Renner	Rare
471	35-60	Liebmann	
472	1-15	Latrobe	
473	16-34	Latrobe	
474	1-15	Latrobe	
475	201-300	Latrobe	
476	136-200	Latrobe	
477	136-200	Latrobe	
478	201-300	Latrobe	
479	201-300	Latrobe	Rare
480	201-300	Latrobe	
481	201-300	Latrobe	Rare/Color
482	61-85	Royal Bohemian	
483	136-200	Jacob Ruppert	
483a	136-200	Jacob Ruppert	
483b	136-200	Jacob Ruppert	
484	35-60	August Schell	
485	201-300	Schiltz	
486	201-300	Schiltz	
487	61-85	Schiltz	
488	86-135	Schiltz	
489	35-60	Schiltz	
490	450+	Schiltz	
491	16-34		Fake
492	450+	Schiltz	Rare
493	16-34	J. Schmidt	
494	1-15	Schmidt (C) & S	
495	16-34	Schmidt (C) & S	
496	61-85	Schmidt (C) & S	
497	16-34	Schmidt (C) & S	
498	35-60	Schmidt (C) & S	
499	61-85	Schmidt (C) & S	

PRICE GUIDE

ITEM NUMBER	PRICE RANGE	BREWERY	COMMENTS
500	35-60	Schmidt (C) & S	
501	61-85	Schoenling	
502	61-85	Schoenling	
503	201-300	Schoenling	Rare
504	301-450	Schott	Rare
505	136-200	Sebewaing	Rare
506	136-200	Sebewaing	Rare
507	136-200	William Simon	Rare
508	35-60	Standard-Rochester	
509	136-200	Sterling	
510	61-85	Sterling	
511	86-135	Sterling	
512	61-85	Sterling	
513	61-85	Sterling	
514	86-135	Jones	
515	136-200	Jones	Rare
516	86-135	Jones	Rare
517	61-85	Jones	
518	61-85	Strohs	
519	61-85	Courage	Rare
520	61-85	Pittsburg	Repainted #521
521	86-135	Pittsburg	
522	16-34	Miller	
523	35-60	Tivoli	
524	86-135	Springfield	Rare
525	35-60	Tivoli	
526	35-60	Carling	
527	61-85	Rochester	
528	201-300	Standard Brewing	Rare
529	61-85	West End	
530	136-200	West End	
531	136-200	West End	
532	35-60	Schmidt (C) & S	
533	61-85	Schmidt (C) & S	
534	61-85	Schmidt (C) & S	
535	450+	Burlington	Rare
536	450+	Burlington	Rare (Authentic?)
537	61-85	Watney	
538	86-135	Watney	
539	136-200	Wehle	Rare
540	136-200	Wehle	Rare
541	35-60		Fake/Novelty

PRICE GUIDE

ITEM NUMBER	PRICE RANGE	BREWERY	COMMENTS
542	136-200	Little Switzerland	
543	136-200	Little Switzerland	
544	136-200	Little Switzerland	
545	201-300	Fessenmeir	
546	201-300	Fessenmeir	Rare
546a	35-60	Fessenmeir	
547	136-200	Whitbread	
548	136-200	Whitbread	
549	35-60	Pacific	
550	1-15	Wooden Shoe	
551	35-60	Minneapolis	
552	450+	Yankee	Rare
553	86-135	Younger	
554	86-135	Pilsen	
555	86-135	Pilsen	
556	136-200	Pilsen	Rare
801	61-85	Acme	
802	61-85	American	
803	61-85	American	
804	86-135	Globe	
805	86-135	Blitz	
806	35-60	North Bay	
807	61-85	Enterprise	
808	61-85	Maier	
809	61-85	Burkhardt	
810	86-135	Burkhardt	
811	61-85	Canadian Ace	
812	35-60	Terre Haute	
813	35-60	Terre Haute	
814	86-135	Oshkosh	
815	61-85	Columbia	
816	61-85	Columbia	
817	61-85	Drewrys	
818	61-85	Drewrys	
819	61-85	Drewrys	
820	61-85	DuBois	
821	35-60	E & B	
822	61-85	E & B	
823	61-85	Jones	
824	86-135	Falls City	

ITEM NUMBER	PRICE RANGE	BREWERY	COMMENTS
825	61-85	Fehr	
826	136-200	Frankenmuth	
827	86-135	Goebel	
828	61-85	Goebel	
829	86-135	Goebel	
830	86-135	Gretz	
831	61-85	Gunther	
832	61-85	Pittsburg	
833	86-135	Kamm's	
834	86-135	Erie	
835	61-85	Erie	
836	61-85	Erie	
837	35-60	Los Angeles	
838	61-85	National	
839	86-135	Eagle	
840	61-85	Cumberland	
841	136-200	Consumers Brewing	
842	86-135	Pilsner	
843	61-85	Lebanon Valley	
844	86-135	Duquesne	
845	61-85	Standard-Rochester	
846	61-85	Weber Waukesha	
847	86-135	Wooden Shoe	
848	86-135	Wooden Shoe	

ITEM NUMBER	PRICE RANGE	BREWERY	COMMENTS